Named as the Abuser

Reactive Abuse, the DARVO Reversal, and How to Reclaim Your Story When You've Been Blamed for Someone Else's Harm

Arnold Wellington McLean

The DARVO Survival Guides, Book 3

Copyright

This book is intended for general informational and educational purposes only. It is not therapy, and it is not legal advice. It is not a substitute for professional psychological, medical, or legal counsel, diagnosis, or treatment, and reading it does not create a therapeutic, legal, or professional relationship of any kind. Only a qualified professional who knows your situation can advise you on it. For decisions about your safety, your relationships, or your legal position, consult a licensed mental health professional, a licensed attorney, or the appropriate authorities in your area.

This book cannot and does not determine the facts of any reader's situation. It offers a way of thinking through a difficult experience, not a verdict on any particular relationship or person. If you are in danger, contact your local emergency services or a domestic abuse helpline.

The author and publisher make no guarantees regarding outcomes. Every situation is different, and results depend on many factors beyond the reach of this book. Readers are responsible for their own decisions and actions.

Disclaimer on case studies. The people in this book are fictional composites. Names are drawn from a fixed, invented set and carry no real identity. The examples are built to illustrate patterns of behavior and are not accounts of any real person, family, or case. Any resemblance to actual individuals or events is coincidental and unintended.

First Edition

ISBN: 979-8-90678-221-2

Staten House

Table of Contents

Preface

Research on manipulation and interpersonal harm has grown sharper over the past two decades, and one pattern has come into clear focus: when a person is confronted about harm they have caused, they often respond not by accounting for it but by turning the confrontation around. The psychologist Jennifer Freyd named this pattern the deny, attack, and reverse victim and offender tactic. Most writing on the subject describes what it does to the person who first spoke up. Far less has been written about what happens when the reversal goes all the way, until the person who was harmed is the one publicly named as the abuser.

That reversal is the subject of this book. It is worth defining precisely, because it is easily confused with two other things. It is not a fair finding that a person did wrong, and it is not the ordinary situation where two people have both behaved badly. It is a specific move in which blame for a pattern of harm is relocated onto the target of that harm, often by seizing on a reaction the harm itself produced. That reaction, sometimes called reactive abuse and more accurately called reactive defense, is one of the tactic's most effective tools, because it manufactures the very evidence it then points to.

The difficulty for the reader in this position is particular. A person of conscience, accused of being the abuser, does not simply reject the charge. They ask whether it is true, and that willingness to question themselves, which distinguishes them from an actual abuser, is exactly what the reversal exploits. Without a fair method for weighing the accusation, they can spend years trapped between denying everything and accepting a false identity whole.

This book supplies that method. It offers a plain self-check for the question of whether the accusation is accurate, a way of reading a relationship through direction, power, and fear rather than isolated incidents, and a set of practical tools for responding to the charge, staying steady when others believe it, and rebuilding trust in one's own character on the ground of evidence. It holds a firm line on genuine accountability throughout, so that owning a real fault and refusing a false whole become separate, manageable acts rather than a single impossible choice.

Named as the Abuser is the third book in The DARVO Survival Guides. The earlier volumes address the reversal as it operates in general and within divorce and custody. This one turns to the reversal aimed at identity, the experience of being cast as the abuser across relationships, families, friendships, and workplaces, and can be read on its own or alongside the others.

The book is written first for the reader who was harmed and then blamed for it, and it will also serve those who support such a reader, along with counselors and advocates who meet this dynamic in their work. It does not diagnose anyone, it cannot determine the facts of any particular situation, and it promises no specific outcome. What it offers is a clear and rigorous way to think through one of the most disorienting experiences a person can face, and to come back to a steady sense of who they are.

Introduction: When the Reversal Has Your Name on It

There is a particular kind of vertigo that comes from being called the abuser by the person who harmed you. It is not the same as being disbelieved, though that is part of it. It is the experience of watching the whole story turn inside out, so that the one who caused the damage becomes the wounded party, and you, the one who was hurt, become the villain of the account. If that has happened to you, whether in a marriage, a family, a friendship, or a workplace, then this book was written for the exact place you are standing.

You may have arrived here carrying a question that will not let you sleep. It is not only, why does no one believe me. It is the more frightening one: what if they are right. What if I am the abusive one. What if the reaction they keep pointing to, the time I yelled, or wept, or slammed a door, or said something cruel, is the real truth about me, and everything else was my excuse. That question is the reason this book takes the shape it does. Reassurance by itself will not settle it, because you are not looking to be comforted. You are looking to know, and then to know what to do.

The pattern that put you here has a name. In the first book of this series, The DARVO Playbook, it is set out in full. DARVO stands for Deny, Attack, and Reverse Victim and Offender. It describes the three moves a person makes when they are confronted with something they did: they deny it, they attack the character of the one raising it, and they reverse the roles so that the wrongdoer appears to be the wronged one. This book is about the sharpest end of that reversal, the moment it stops being merely a way to avoid blame and becomes a way to pin the blame on you, to make you, in the eyes of others and sometimes in your own eyes, the abuser.

I want to be careful and clear about what this book will and will not do, because the subject demands it. This book will help you understand why you were cast in this role, tell the difference between a reaction to harm and a pattern of harm, answer the accusation in a way that protects rather than confirms it, repair anything that genuinely is yours to repair, and rebuild trust in your own character. It will not diagnose the other person, and it will discourage you from trying to, because a label you cannot prove tends to hurt you more than it helps. It will not give you a verdict on your particular situation, because no book can know your life. And it will not offer you an easy way to dodge responsibility, because that would betray both you and the people this book is truly for.

That last point deserves its own paragraph, spoken plainly. A tactic like the reversal can be run by anyone, and a person who has genuinely caused harm can pick up a book like this and look for permission. This book refuses to give it. The material here is built to help the person who was harmed and then blamed, and it holds a firm line: understanding a reaction is not the same as excusing it, and owning a real fault is not the same as accepting a false identity. If you are willing to look at your own conduct with courage, you will find that this book helps you see clearly. If you are looking only for a way to feel innocent without examining anything, you will find that it keeps asking you to look again. That tension is deliberate, and it is what makes the clarity on the other side worth trusting.

Here is what is within your reach, whatever was said about you. You cannot control the accusation, and you cannot force the other person to take it back. You can understand the tactic, examine the question fairly and reach an answer you can stand on, respond in ways that keep your footing, and come back to a grounded sense of who you actually are. The accusation was loud. Your steady self-knowledge can be steadier.

Before we begin, write down one sentence: the accusation as it was actually put to you, in the words that were used. Keep it nearby. We are going to take it apart, weigh it fairly, and by the end you will know what to do with it. Name the tactic, and reclaim your story.

Chapter 1: The Reversal Lands on You

Avenor said one true sentence, and it cost them everything. They were thirty-nine, and after two years of a friendship that had slowly curdled into something controlling, they finally said the quiet thing out loud: that their friend's behavior had been hurting them, and it needed to change. They said it carefully, without cruelty, in the way you rehearse a hard sentence for weeks before you dare to speak it. What came back was not an apology, and it was not even a denial exactly. It was a reversal so complete that within a month Avenor was the one being described, to their whole shared circle, as manipulative, controlling, and abusive. The friend wept to others about how much Avenor had hurt them. Avenor, who had finally found the courage to name harm, was now the named one, and the word attached to them was the very word they had been trying to speak.

That is the experience this book is about, and this chapter is where we give it a name and a shape. Being cast as the abuser is not the same as being disagreed with, and it is not the same as being disbelieved. It is a specific move, the last and sharpest move of a recognizable tactic, and understanding it as a tactic rather than as a verdict on your character is the first thing that will steady the ground under you. You cannot respond well to something you cannot yet see clearly, and right now the accusation may be so large and so loud that it fills your whole field of vision. We are going to step back far enough to see its shape.

The reversal has your name on it

The principle to hold at the start is this: the reversal has your name on it, but that does not make the name true. Jennifer Freyd described the pattern in nineteen ninety-seven, and named its three moves:

deny, attack, and reverse victim and offender (Freyd, 1997). The first two moves are familiar to anyone who has confronted a person unwilling to be accountable. The denial rewrites what happened. The attack goes after your character so that the subject changes from the deed to your worth. It is the third move, the reversal, that this book lives inside, because when it succeeds fully, it does not merely deflect the blame. It relocates it, onto you, and it does so with such conviction that the roles appear to swap in the eyes of everyone watching, and sometimes in your own eyes as well.

This matters because it tells you what you are actually facing. You are not facing a fair account of your conduct that you must now disprove. You are facing a move, a predictable and studied move, whose entire purpose is to make the person who caused harm appear to be its victim. When you see it as a move, you stop treating the accusation as a mirror and start treating it as a maneuver. That shift does not make the pain smaller, but it changes what the pain means. The label is not information about who you are. It is information about what is being done to you.

Why the wronged one so often becomes the accused

There is a cruel logic to why the person who was harmed is so frequently the one who ends up named as the abuser, and understanding it will spare you a great deal of self-blame. Consider who is likely to react visibly. The person being subjected to sustained control or cruelty is under enormous pressure, and pressure produces reactions: raised voices, tears, sharp words, a door closed too hard. The person applying the pressure, by contrast, is often composed, because they are not the one being crushed. When an outside observer arrives late to the scene, they see one person distraught and one person calm, and the distraught one looks, on the surface, like the problem.

The reversal exploits exactly this. It waits for or provokes a reaction, and then presents that reaction, stripped of everything that produced it, as the true face of the accused. Your months of restraint are invisible. Your ten seconds of breaking are the exhibit. And because the person running the reversal is practiced at appearing reasonable, the contrast does the work for them. This is not a sign that you are weak or that observers are stupid. It is a structural feature of how harm and reaction look from the outside, and the reversal is built to take advantage of it.

An accusation is not a conviction

Hold on to a distinction that the coming chapters will develop and that you will need on the hard nights: an accusation is not the same as the truth of your conduct. Being called the abuser is an event that happened to you. Whether you actually behaved abusively is a separate question, one that deserves a careful and fair examination rather than a panicked surrender. Many people, in the first shock of the accusation, collapse the two together. They reason that if they are being called abusive, and if they did once react badly, then the accusation must be true and they must be a monster. That collapse is the reversal working exactly as intended, because it needs you to accept the label without weighing it.

We will weigh it properly in the chapters ahead, and we will not flinch from the possibility that some of the accusation contains something real. But the weighing is a process, not a reflex, and it cannot be done in the grip of the first terror. For now, simply refuse the collapse. The accusation is a claim. Claims can be examined. You are permitted to set the claim down on the table and look at it, rather than swallowing it whole.

How the label spreads

Part of what makes this experience so disorienting is how quickly the label travels. The person running the reversal rarely keeps it private.

They tell friends, family, colleagues, sometimes anyone who will listen, and they tell it well, because a convincing performance of victimhood is part of the tactic. By the time you understand what is happening, the story may already be established in a dozen minds, and you are left in the position of trying to disprove a thing that has hardened into common knowledge. This is why so many people in your position describe feeling as though the ground moved while they were looking elsewhere.

Understanding that the spread is a feature, not an accident, helps you respond to it wisely later. The reversal seeks an audience because an audience makes the reversed story feel true and leaves you isolated, which is a subject we will take up in full. For now, the point is only to see the mechanism clearly. The speed and reach of the accusation are not evidence that it is true. They are evidence that the tactic is working, and the tactic works partly by moving fast.

Why a name steadies you

There is real power in having a name for what is happening to you, and it is worth pausing on why. When an experience has no name, it tends to attach itself to your identity: this is happening because of who I am, because of something wrong in me. When the experience has a name, and especially when that name describes a pattern that has happened to many others, it detaches from your identity and becomes a thing with a shape, a cause, and a set of responses. Avenor described the moment they learned the word reversal as the first breath they had taken in months, not because it fixed anything, but because it moved the problem from inside their character to outside it, where it could be seen and handled.

That is what this chapter offers before anything else: the name, and the shape. You have not been handed a fair verdict that you must now accept. You have been subjected to the sharp end of a recognizable tactic, one whose purpose is to make the harmed party carry the blame. The rest of this book is about what to do with that knowledge, but the knowledge itself is the first foothold. Avenor's story does not end here with vindication, because at this stage there was none to be had, and pretending otherwise would fail you. It ends with something more useful: they stopped asking what was wrong with them and started asking what was being done to them, and that question, unlike the first, had answers.

What the reversal needs from you

It is worth naming what the reversal actually requires in order to succeed, because once you see it, you can decline to supply it. The tactic needs two things from you specifically. It needs your reaction, the visible break it can point to, and it needs your collapse, the moment you accept the label and begin to believe you are what you have been called. The first it will often provoke. The second it depends on you handing over freely, in the privacy of your own mind, on the nights when the accusation feels heaviest.

This is oddly good news, because both of those things are, at least in part, within your control. You can learn to regulate the reaction, which is the work of a later chapter, and you can refuse the collapse, which begins right now. Refusing the collapse does not mean insisting on your own innocence before you have examined anything. It means holding the question open rather than answering it in terror. The person running the reversal is counting on your terror to close the question in their favor. Every time you keep it open long enough to look, you take back a piece of ground the tactic needed you to surrender.

Two kinds of readers, one clear test

I said in the introduction that a book like this can be picked up by two very different people, and this chapter is the right place to make the distinction sharp, because it protects you. One reader was harmed and then blamed, and is tormented by the fear that the blame might be deserved. The other caused harm and is looking for a way to feel like the victim without changing anything. The strange thing is that both may recognize themselves in the opening pages, because the reversal is a real tactic and can be claimed falsely as easily as it can be described truly.

The test that separates them is not comfort but willingness. The genuinely harmed reader is usually the one most willing to examine themselves, most afraid of being unfair, most ready to own a real fault. The person misusing the frame is usually the one least willing to look, quickest to place all blame elsewhere, most eager for a verdict of innocence that requires no self-examination. This book is built around that test. It will keep asking you to look at your own conduct with courage, and it will treat your willingness to do so as meaningful. If that willingness is in you, the accusation you are carrying is already less likely to be the truth than the terror insists, and the chapters ahead will help you see why. Hold that as a small, steadying light: the very fact that you are afraid you might be the abuser is not the behavior of the thing you are afraid of being.

Trying it on your own situation

Begin to build the clarity this book depends on, gently and on real material.

First, take the sentence you wrote at the end of the introduction, the accusation in the words that were used, and separate two things in writing: what you were called, and what you actually did. Keep them in two columns. The gap between them is where this book does its work.

Second, for that same accusation, find the three moves if they are present: the denial of what really happened, the attack on your character, and the reversal that made you the offender. Naming the moves trains you to see the tactic instead of only feeling the wound.

Third, write one sentence of orientation to keep nearby: I was named the abuser, and being named is not the same as being it, so I am going to weigh this fairly rather than swallow it whole. That sentence is the posture of the entire book.

Fourth, notice, without judging it, the moment your mind collapses the accusation into a verdict. For a few days, simply catch the thought when it comes, the one that says the label must be true because it was spoken with such certainty, and mark it as the collapse the tactic needs. You do not have to argue with it yet. You only have to notice that it is a move being made inside you, not a conclusion you reasoned your way to. Seeing the collapse as a reflex rather than a finding is the beginning of getting free of it.

A closing word for the hardest nights, because this chapter names a wound that throbs worst in the dark. If you are lying awake asking whether you are the monster they described, hold this: that question, asked with that much fear, is not the question a monster asks. It is the question of someone with a conscience, turned against themselves by a tactic built to do exactly that. You are permitted to set the question down until morning, when you can look at it in better light with the tools this book will give you. The accusation will still be there to examine. So will you, and you are steadier than the night makes you feel. Morning has a way of shrinking what the dark makes enormous, and the work of this book is done in daylight, with a clear head and a fair method, not in the small hours when the accusation has the room to itself.

Where this leaves you

Being cast as the abuser is the sharpest end of the deny, attack, reverse tactic, the move that does not merely deflect blame but relocates it onto you (Freyd, 1997). The wronged party is so often the one accused because harm produces visible reactions while control can stay composed, and the reversal presents the reaction, stripped of context, as the truth. An accusation is not a conviction; it is a claim you are permitted to examine rather than swallow, and the speed with which the label spreads is evidence that the tactic is working, not that it is true. A name for the experience moves it from inside your character to outside it, where it can be handled. The most frightening part of this experience is the question it plants, whether the accusation might be true, and the next chapters face that question directly, beginning with the reaction that was turned into the evidence against you.

Chapter 2: Reactive Defense, Not Reactive Abuse

Maevren has one memory she cannot stop replaying, and it is ten seconds long. She was thirty-four, and for the better part of a year her partner had been narrating a version of her back to her that she did not recognize: cold, ungrateful, unstable. On the night in question, he had been at it for hours, following her from room to room, calm and relentless, listing her failures, until something in her that had held for months finally gave way, and she screamed at him to stop and threw a cup, which shattered against the wall. He had his phone out before the pieces settled. He filmed her standing there, shaking and crying, and that ten seconds, her worst ten seconds, became the clip he showed to others as proof of who she really was. The hours that produced it were nowhere in the frame.

This chapter is about that ten seconds, and about the thousands of people who carry a version of it: the moment they reacted, and watched the reaction become the whole story. It is the most delicate material in this book, and it must be handled with care in two directions at once. On one side, a reaction to sustained harm is not the same as a pattern of harm, and treating it as though it were is a cruelty that compounds the original one. On the other side, a reaction can still be something you regret and something you own, and pretending otherwise would make this book useless and untruthful. We are going to hold both of those truths, because the clarity you need lives exactly where they meet.

A reaction is not the pattern

The principle of this chapter is that a reaction is not the pattern. When a person is subjected to ongoing control, provocation, or cruelty, the body and mind eventually respond, and the response can look, in a single frame, like aggression. Advocates and clinicians have a term for this, reactive abuse, and it names something real, but the term itself carries a problem that you should see clearly. To call a harmed person's reaction abuse is to hand the reversal its language, because it quietly relocates the label of abuser onto the one who was defending themselves. For that reason many who work in this area prefer the term reactive defense, which describes the same event more accurately: a defensive response to ongoing harm, not a fresh act of abuse originating in the person who reacted.

The distinction is not a word game. It changes what you understand about yourself. If your reaction was reactive abuse, then you are, in some measure, an abuser who was provoked. If it was reactive defense, then you are a person under sustained pressure who responded, at last, in a way you may not be proud of, but which did not originate the harm and does not define your character. The truth of most cases described in this book is far closer to the second than to the first, and learning to see your own reaction in that more accurate light is part of what loosens the accusation's grip.

How sustained pressure produces a reaction

It helps to understand the mechanism, because understanding it removes some of the shame. Sustained control and provocation work on the nervous system. A person who is criticized, denied, and pressured over long periods lives in a state of chronic threat, and a body held in threat for long enough will eventually discharge that tension, sometimes explosively, sometimes in tears, sometimes in a single sharp act that is entirely out of character for the calm person underneath. This is not a character flaw revealing itself. It is a predictable response of a pressured system, and it is one of the reasons coercive control is so corrosive: it manufactures the very reactions it then points to as proof (Stark, 2007).

Seen this way, the reaction is better understood as a symptom of what was being done to you than as evidence of what you are. This does not make the reaction disappear, and it does not automatically excuse everything a person might do under pressure. But it reframes the reaction from a window into your true nature to a mark left by sustained harm. Maevren did not throw a cup because she was violent. She threw a cup because a calm man had followed her through her own home for hours, and a body can only hold so much. The cup was the evidence he wanted. The hours were the truth he hid.

Captured and presented out of context

The reversal does not merely wait for a reaction; it often engineers and captures one. This is worth naming plainly, because many people carry deep shame about a reaction that was, in fact, deliberately provoked and deliberately recorded. The pattern is consistent across many accounts: the person applying pressure escalates until the harmed person breaks, and then produces the break, sometimes on video, sometimes simply in a vivid retelling, as the definitive proof of who the accused really is. The context, the hours or months or years that produced the reaction, is precisely what gets removed, because the reaction only works as evidence once it is stripped of its cause.

When you understand this, a reframe becomes available that can lift an enormous weight. The clip, the story, the moment they keep pointing to, was designed to look like the whole picture while showing almost none of it. You are not obligated to accept a single frame as the summary of a long ordeal. This does not mean you refuse to look at your own reaction, which we will do carefully. It means you refuse to accept the reversal's editing of your life, in which the cause is deleted and only the symptom remains on screen.

The line you must still hold

Here is where care in the other direction becomes essential, and where this book parts company with anything that would let a genuine wrongdoer off the hook. Reactive defense explains a reaction; it does not license every possible action, and it does not turn a pattern of harm into innocence. There is a limit to what pressure can account for. A reaction that reaches for a weapon, that targets a child, that becomes its own sustained campaign of cruelty, has passed beyond defense into harm of its own, whatever provoked it, and no reader is served by a book that blurs that boundary. Naming the boundary protects the very readers this book is for, because it means that when you conclude your reaction was defensive, the conclusion actually means something. There is a difference between a person who, after months of provocation, finally shouted or wept or threw something, and a person who repeatedly frightens, controls, or injures another and then calls it a reaction. The first is reactive defense. The second is a pattern of harm wearing the costume of reactive defense, and the clear-eyed reader must be willing to tell them apart in their own life.

This is why the next chapter follows, and why this one refuses to end on pure reassurance. If you are willing to ask whether your reaction was a defensive break under sustained pressure or part of a pattern of harm you have been minimizing, you are doing the work that makes your self-understanding trustworthy. Most readers of this book, having done that work, will find that their reaction was defensive, and that the pattern of harm ran the other way. But the finding has to be earned by looking, not assumed, and the willingness to look is itself one of the clearest signs that the reversal, not your character, is the real problem here.

The trap of the mutual abuse claim

One of the most disorienting forms this takes is the claim that the relationship was mutually abusive, that both of you were equally at fault, that it takes two. On its surface this can sound fair and even generous, and sometimes, rarely, it names something real. But in the hands of the reversal it is a precise tool, because it takes a one-directional pattern of control and reframes it as a symmetrical fight between two equally responsible parties. Once the situation is called mutual, your reactive defense and their sustained harm are placed on the same scale, as though a person crying and throwing a cup after hours of pressure were the equal of the person who applied the pressure.

The way through the mutual abuse claim is not to insist reflexively that you did nothing wrong, which no fair-minded person can say of any long conflict, but to look at direction, power, and fear, which the next chapters develop in full. Ask who was generally afraid of whom. Ask who controlled the terms of the relationship and who was adapting to survive them. Ask which behavior originated and which responded. Abuse is not simply the presence of bad moments on both sides; it is a pattern of power and control running predominantly in one direction. When you hold the mutual abuse claim up against that understanding, you can often see that what is being called symmetry is actually a single direction of harm with your reaction bolted on as false evidence of balance.

When shame does the reversal's work

There is a particular emotion this chapter must address directly, because it can undo everything else, and that emotion is shame. The reaction you are ashamed of has a way of becoming, in your own mind, the proof of your guilt, so that you finish the reversal's work in the privacy of your own conscience long after the other person has stopped speaking. You replay the ten seconds. You feel the heat of it. And the shame whispers that a good person would never have done that, so you must not be a good person, so the accusation must be right. This is the reversal completed from the inside, and it is why shame, left unexamined, is so dangerous here.

The answer to this shame is not to pretend the reaction did not happen or did not matter. It is to place the reaction back into its true proportion. A single break, or even several, under sustained harm, is a human response to being harmed, not the defining fact of your character. You are allowed to regret the reaction and to refuse the identity in the same breath. Maevren spent a year believing the cup was the truest thing about her. What began to free her was not forgetting it, but restoring it to scale: one bad moment inside a long ordeal, regrettable and human, and nowhere near large enough to be the whole of who she was. Shame wants the reaction to be everything. Accuracy insists it is one thing, in context, among many.

Trying it on your own situation

This chapter's practice asks you to look at a painful memory with new eyes, and to do it with fairness in both directions.

First, write out the reaction you are most ashamed of, the one they point to, in full. Then, above it, write the context that produced it: what came before, for how long, and at whose hand. Seeing the cause restored to the symptom is the core work of this chapter.

Second, ask two questions of that reaction in writing. Did this response originate the harm, or respond to it. And is this a rare break under pressure, or a recurring way I treat this person. Your answers begin to tell you whether you are looking at reactive defense or something you need to take up in the accountability chapter.

Third, practice describing the event in the more accurate language: not I was abusive, but I reached my limit after sustained harm and reacted in a way I regret. Notice that this sentence owns the reaction without accepting the false identity. That is the balance this whole book is built to help you hold.

Fourth, if the mutual abuse claim has been used against you, write the pattern out along the three markers named above: direction, power, and fear. For a set of specific incidents, note who originated the behavior, who held the power in the moment, and who was afraid. Do not force the answers; let the pattern show itself across several examples. Many readers find that what was called a two-sided fight resolves, on paper, into a single direction of control with their own reactions scattered through it as the only evidence of balance. That is worth seeing clearly, because the mutual abuse claim loses much of its power once you can describe the actual shape of what happened. A named shape is something you can stand on. A vague sense that maybe it was all your fault is something that swallows you. Moving from the second to the first is much of the work of this book.

A closing reassurance, offered with care. This chapter has asked you to look at your worst moment, which is hard, and to look at it fairly, which is harder. Please be gentle with yourself in the looking. The goal is not to excuse yourself and it is not to condemn yourself; it is to see accurately, because accuracy is what the reversal has been working to destroy. If restoring your reaction to its true proportion is more than you can do on your own, that is not a failure, and a skilled professional can help you hold both the regret and the context without collapsing into either. You reacted because you were being harmed. That sentence is not an excuse. It is, for most readers of this book, simply the truth, and the truth is where recovery begins. For most people who were harmed and then blamed, that truth is kinder than the accusation, though it may not feel that way until you have looked at it squarely and in steady company.

What to carry forward

A reaction is not the pattern. When a person is subjected to sustained control and provocation, the pressured nervous system eventually discharges, and that discharge can look, in a single frame, like aggression while being, in truth, a defensive response to ongoing harm (Stark, 2007). The common term reactive abuse quietly hands the reversal its language, which is why reactive defense is often the more accurate name. The reversal frequently provokes and captures the reaction, then presents it stripped of the context that produced it, and you are not obligated to accept that editing of your life. And yet the line must hold in the other direction: reactive defense explains a reaction without licensing a pattern of harm, and the willingness to tell those apart in your own life is exactly what makes your self-understanding trustworthy. That willingness leads directly into the hardest question in this book, the one the next chapter faces without flinching: am I the abuser.

Chapter 3: The Question You Cannot Avoid, Am I the Abuser

Isoren almost did not survive the question, and he was not being dramatic when he said so. He was forty-three, and months after his marriage ended he was still lying awake with the same sentence circling: what if she was right, what if I am the abuser. He had been the one belittled and controlled for years, and he knew that, and yet he had also, near the end, done things he was not proud of. He had shouted. Once he had blocked a doorway so she could not walk away from an argument. The accusation she made, that he was the abusive one, kept finding those moments and holding them up as proof, and Isoren could not tell anymore whether he was a victim who had reacted or a perpetrator who had been caught. The not knowing was destroying him. This chapter is the one he needed, and it is the ethical center of this book.

Everything in these pages has been building toward this question, because it is the question underneath all the others. Not whether others believe the accusation, but whether it is true. Am I the abuser. I am not going to answer it for you, because I cannot know your life, and because a book that simply reassured you would be worthless to a person genuinely trying to see clearly. What I can give you is a way to ask the question rigorously and fairly, so that you reach an answer you have earned and can stand on, rather than an answer handed to you by terror or by the person who accused you.

Ask it plainly, and mean it

The principle of this chapter is to ask the question plainly and to mean it. Most people in your position do one of two things with the question, and both fail. Some refuse it entirely, insisting on their innocence so fiercely that they never look, which leaves the doubt alive underneath, unexamined and powerful. Others surrender to it completely, deciding they must be the monster because they cannot bear the uncertainty, which hands the reversal its victory. The third way, the one this chapter teaches, is to hold the question open long enough to examine it with a fair method, and then to reach a grounded conclusion. This is harder than either denial or surrender, and it is the only path that leads somewhere you can actually live.

To ask it plainly, you have to be willing to find either answer. That willingness is the whole thing. If you approach the question determined to prove your innocence, you are not really asking it. If you approach it certain of your guilt, you are not asking it either. You are asking it only when you can say, truthfully, that you want to know what is real, whichever way it falls. That posture is rare, and it is also the posture least likely to belong to an actual abuser, who typically cannot tolerate the question at all. The fact that you are willing to sit inside it is already meaningful, though it is not yet the answer.

The accountability self-check

Here is a set of questions to ask before you conclude anything about the accusation. They are drawn from the earlier books in this series and sharpened for this situation. Run them in writing, slowly, on the specific accusation you are facing.

First, am I willing to find that some of this is true. If no part of the accusation could ever be valid in your eyes, that total defensiveness is worth examining, because it can be its own kind of refusal to look.

Second, does the accusation name specific behaviors I actually did, or does it mostly attack my character. A specific, checkable behavior deserves a careful look. A wall of character attack, with no concrete conduct behind it, is often the shape of a reversal rather than a reckoning.

Third, when I did react badly, did my behavior originate the harm or respond to it. This is the reactive defense question from the previous chapter, and it is central. A response to sustained harm is a different thing from a campaign of harm, even when the surface behavior looks similar.

Fourth, is there a pattern of me controlling, frightening, or coercing this person over time, or are there moments of me reacting inside a pattern where they controlled or frightened me. Abuse is a pattern of power, not a collection of bad moments, and the direction of the pattern is what matters most.

Fifth, who was generally afraid of whom. Fear is one of the most reliable signals of the direction of harm, and it is hard to fake to yourself in the quiet of your own reflection.

Run these five questions with courage, and they will sort most situations. They will also, for a small number of readers, surface something that needs to be owned, and if that is you, the later chapter on genuine repair is written for exactly that. The point of the check is not to deliver a comfortable verdict. It is to deliver a true one.

Why willingness is evidence

There is a finding from the research on this tactic that speaks directly to your situation and that you should carry with you. When people are confronted about harm they have caused, those who use the reversal tend to respond with denial, attack, and role-reversal, and exposure to that pattern is associated with increased self-blame in the people they are confronting (Harsey, Zurbriggen, & Freyd, 2017). Read that carefully, because it describes what may have happened to you. The self-blame you are drowning in, the very question am I the abuser, is a known effect of having the reversal used against you. It is, in a real sense, a symptom of what was done to you, not a reliable readout of what you did.

This is why your willingness to examine yourself is meaningful rather than incidental. The person running a reversal is characterized precisely by their unwillingness to be accountable; that unwillingness is the engine of the whole tactic. Your torment over whether you might be the abuser is the near-opposite of that unwillingness. Research on self-compassion suggests, further, that people who can meet their own failures with care rather than with harsh self-attack are more able to take genuine responsibility, not less, because they are not fighting to protect a fragile self-image (Neff, 2003). The cruelty you are aiming at yourself is not making you more accountable. It is making you less able to see straight. A steadier, kinder rigor will serve the truth better than self-punishment ever could.

A word to the reader who fears the check will condemn them

Some readers approach this self-check terrified that it will confirm the worst, and that fear can make them avoid it, or run it in bad faith, tilting every answer toward guilt to punish themselves or toward innocence to escape. It is worth saying clearly that the check is not a trap and it is not a trial. It is a light. Its purpose is not to convict you and not to acquit you, but to let you see what is actually there, which is the one thing the reversal has worked hardest to prevent.

If you find that running the questions truthfully is more than you can bear on your own, that is not a weakness, and it is a strong reason to bring a skilled professional into the process. A good therapist can hold the questions with you, steady you when an answer frightens you, and help you tell the difference between the voice of genuine conscience and the voice the reversal installed. There is no virtue in doing this in isolation, and for many readers the self-check is best run not as a solitary ordeal but as work done alongside someone trained to help. Reaching for that help is part of taking the question seriously, not a way of avoiding it.

Why fear points the way

Of the five questions, the one about fear deserves special attention, because it is the hardest to deceive yourself about and the most revealing. Abuse, at bottom, is about power and control, and control produces fear in the person being controlled. So the question of who was afraid of whom, asked across the whole span of the relationship rather than about a single incident, tends to cut through confusion faster than any other. A person who spent years managing their words and movements to avoid another's anger, who felt relief when the other left the room, who monitored moods to stay safe, was living in fear, and fear of that kind runs in the direction of harm.

Ask it in both directions and be truthful. Were there times the other person seemed afraid of you. If so, look at those squarely and take them into the repair chapter if they were real. But then ask the larger question: across the years, who lived in a state of watchfulness and fear, and who held the power that produced it. For most readers of this book, the answer, once faced, is clear, and it is not the answer the accusation insists on. Fear is difficult to fake to yourself in the quiet of reflection, which is exactly why it is such a reliable guide to the direction of harm, and why the reversal works so hard to keep you from asking the question at all.

The two lists that keep you sane

If there is one habit to take from this chapter, it is the discipline of keeping two lists rather than one verdict. On the first list go the things you genuinely did that you need to own: the shout, the blocked doorway, the cruel sentence, whatever the courageous check surfaced as real. On the second list go the things you are being blamed for that are not yours: the false character verdict, the reversal of who harmed whom, the pattern of control that ran the other way. Most people, in the grip of the accusation, refuse to make two lists, because they feel that admitting anything onto the first list proves the second. It does not, and the refusal to separate them is what keeps them trapped.

The two lists are what let you be both accountable and free. The first list is where your integrity lives; you will take it into the repair chapter and act on it. The second list is where your self-respect lives; you will refuse it, steadily, no matter how loudly it is asserted. Isoren kept his two lists on a single page, folded in a drawer, and when the doubt came for him he would take it out and read both columns, and the reading did what argument never could. It reminded him that he was a person with real faults and real limits, not a monster and not a saint, which is the truth about nearly everyone, and a truth the reversal is specifically built to erase.

Reaching an answer you can stand on

The goal of the self-check is a conclusion you can return to when the doubt surges again, as it will. Write it down when you reach it, in plain words, because a written conclusion made in a clear moment is something you can hold on to in an unclear one. For most readers who do this work with courage, the conclusion sounds something like this: I did some things I regret, and I have named them and will repair what can be repaired, and I was not the origin or the pattern of harm in this relationship, and I am not the abuser they called me. That sentence owns what is real and refuses what is false, and it is the sentence this entire book is trying to help you earn.

Isoren reached his version of it slowly. He owned the shouting and the blocked doorway, named them clearly, and did not minimize them. And he also saw, running the check, that these were reactions inside years of being controlled, that the fear in the relationship had run overwhelmingly one direction, and that the pattern of harm was not his. He was not innocent of everything, and he was not the abuser. Both were true, and holding both was what finally let him sleep. His conclusion did not make him comfortable. It made him clear, and clarity, not comfort, is what this chapter is for.

Trying it on your own situation

This practice is uncomfortable on purpose, because a conclusion you can trust has to be earned by looking.

First, run all five self-check questions in writing on your specific accusation. Answer the fourth and fifth with particular care, because pattern and fear are the most telling.

Second, complete this sentence as truthfully as you can: the things I genuinely need to own are, and the things I refuse to accept are. Keeping the two lists separate is the core skill of this book.

Third, write your grounded conclusion in one or two plain sentences, and keep it where you can reach it. When the doubt returns at night, you will not have to run the whole examination again; you will have your earned answer already written, in your own hand, from a clearer hour.

Fourth, if the check surfaced something genuinely yours to own, do not spiral and do not flee. Write it plainly on a separate line, mark it as work for the repair chapter, and set it down for now. Owning a real fault is not the same as accepting the accusation, and treating it as such is the all-or-nothing trap the later chapter dismantles. Keeping your genuine faults in one place and the false label in another is what lets you be accountable without being crushed, and that separation is a skill you can practice starting today.

A closing word, because this is the chapter that decides so much. The question am I the abuser has driven good people to despair, and it has done so precisely because they were good enough to ask it. If you have run the check with courage and reached a conclusion that owns your real faults and refuses the false whole, you have done something the person who accused you almost certainly cannot do, and that difference is not nothing. It is close to everything. Carry your written conclusion the way you would carry a light into a dark room. The dark will return, but the light is yours now, and you made it yourself, out of courage and a fair method, which is the only kind of answer that can truly hold.

Where this leaves you

The question underneath all the others is whether the accusation is true, and the only path that leads somewhere livable is to hold it open long enough to examine it fairly, then reach a grounded conclusion. Ask it plainly and mean it, willing to find either answer, using the five-question self-check of willingness, specific behavior, origin, pattern, and fear. Your very torment over the question is, according to the research, a known effect of having the reversal used against you rather than a readout of guilt, and self-punishment makes you less able to see clearly, not more (Harsey, Zurbriggen, & Freyd, 2017; Neff, 2003). Reach an answer you can stand on, one that owns what is real and refuses what is false, and write it down for the hard hours. Having faced the question, the next chapter explains why the doubt felt so overwhelmingly true in the first place, so that you can loosen its grip for good.

Chapter 4: Why the Doubt Feels So True

Solenne could recite the accusation in her sleep, because it had become the voice in her own head. She was thirty-seven, two years out of a relationship that had slowly rewritten her, and the strange thing she noticed was that she no longer needed her former partner in the room to feel worthless. The sentences he had used, that she was selfish, that she was the toxic one, that everyone would see through her eventually, now arrived on their own, in her own inner voice, unprompted, at the smallest provocation. She would make an ordinary decision and hear, that is exactly the kind of selfish thing he always said you do. The accusation had moved in. It no longer needed an accuser, because it had become part of how she talked to herself.

This chapter is about that migration, the way the accusation gets inside you and starts to feel like the truth spoken by your own judgment rather than a claim made by someone else. Understanding how the doubt was installed is what allows you to loosen its grip, because a doubt you believe is your own insight is nearly impossible to argue with, while a doubt you can recognize as an implanted echo begins, slowly, to lose its authority. The goal of this chapter is not to talk you out of the doubt by force, which does not work, but to help you see where it came from, so that you can stop mistaking it for your own clear sight.

The voice was installed

The principle here is that the voice was installed. The self-doubt you are living with did not arise from an accurate reading of your own character. It was placed in you, deliberately or through sustained repetition, by someone who benefited from your doubting yourself. This is not a metaphor. When a person hears, day after day, that they are selfish, unstable, or abusive, from someone whose approval or love they depend on, the mind begins to absorb the claim, not because it is true, but because the mind under sustained pressure looks for a way to make the pain make sense, and self-blame is often the path of least resistance. It is easier, in a strange way, to believe you are the problem than to fully face that someone you trusted was harming you.

Seeing the voice as installed changes your relationship to it. You do not have to win an argument with your own worthlessness, which is a fight no one wins. You have to recognize a particular thought as an implant, a line of dialogue written by someone else and left running in your head. When Solenne learned to hear the selfish sentence and think, that is his voice, not mine, the sentence did not vanish, but it lost its status as truth. It became a quotation rather than a verdict, and a quotation can be set down.

Why betrayal makes us doubt ourselves

There is a reason the mind tilts toward self-blame under this kind of harm, and it runs deep. When the person harming you is someone you depend on or trusted, your mind faces an unbearable conflict, because fully recognizing the betrayal threatens the attachment you may still need or grieve. Research on betrayal describes how, in exactly these conditions, awareness can bend away from the betrayal and toward self-doubt, because doubting yourself preserves the relationship in your mind while facing the betrayal would shatter it (Freyd, 1996). Self-blame, in other words, is not a sign of weak character. It is a protective response of a mind trying to survive a betrayal by someone it could not afford to lose.

This is worth sitting with, because it reframes the very self-doubt that torments you. The fact that you turned the harm inward, that you asked what is wrong with me rather than what is being done to me, is not evidence that you were the problem. It is evidence that you were in a betrayal bind, and that your mind did what minds do to survive one. The doubt feels true partly because it once served a purpose, holding a necessary relationship together at the cost of your own self-trust. Now that the relationship is over or exposed, the doubt has outlived its function, but it goes on running, which is why it can feel so real long after the accuser is gone.

Gaslighting and the erosion of your perception

Layered on top of the betrayal bind is often a more deliberate process, the sustained undermining of your confidence in your own perceptions. Gaslighting, the effort to make a person doubt their own memory and judgment, wears down over time the very faculty you would need to evaluate the accusation. Its effects are not only private and psychological; they draw on differences in power and on social realities that make the target more likely to doubt themselves and less likely to be believed (Sweet, 2019). When you have been told for years that you remember wrong, overreact, and misread situations, you arrive at the accusation with your instrument for judging it already damaged.

This produces a cruel loop that you should be able to name. The accusation says you are the abuser. The tool you would use to assess that claim, your own perception, has been systematically undermined by the same person making the claim. So you reach for your judgment and find it unreliable, which the accuser has ensured, and in that unreliability the accusation flourishes. Naming this loop is part of breaking it. Your uncertainty about your own perception is not a neutral fact about your unreliable mind. It is, in large part, a result that was produced in you, and recognizing it as a produced result rather than a true limitation is what lets you begin to trust yourself again.

Feeling like the abuser is not being one

Out of all of this comes a single sentence that many readers need to hear and write down: feeling like the abuser is not the same as being one. The reversal, the betrayal bind, and the gaslighting together manufacture a feeling of guilt and badness that is disconnected from your actual conduct. You can feel monstrous and have behaved, on the whole, like a person under sustained harm who reacted at times. The feeling is real, but it is not reliable evidence, because it was produced by the very forces this chapter has described, and produced feelings do not track truth.

This is precisely why the self-check of the previous chapter matters so much. You cannot trust the feeling, so you need a method that does not rely on the feeling. The five questions of the self-check are that method, a way to reach a conclusion about your conduct that does not depend on how guilty you happen to feel in the afternoon or in the small hours. When the installed feeling surges and tells you that you are the abuser, you do not have to argue with the feeling. You can return to your written conclusion, reached by method in a clearer hour, and let it outrank the feeling, because a conclusion reached by fair examination is more trustworthy than a feeling manufactured by a tactic.

Why arguing with the doubt does not work

Many people try to defeat the installed voice by argument, marshaling evidence of their own goodness, listing their kind acts, reasoning with the worthlessness as though it could be persuaded. It rarely works, and it helps to understand why, so you stop exhausting yourself in a fight you cannot win that way. The installed voice does not run on logic, so logic does not reach it. It was placed by repetition and emotion, in conditions of pressure and fear, and it lives in a part of you that does not respond to a well-constructed case. You can prove to yourself on paper that you are not what you were called, and still feel, an hour later, exactly as monstrous as before.

What works better is not argument but recognition and repetition of a different kind. Recognition means labeling the voice as installed each time it speaks, which slowly changes your relationship to it even when it does not silence it. Repetition means living, over months, in conditions of safety and steadiness where the old voice is no longer being reinforced by a present accuser, so that it gradually fades for lack of fuel. The voice was built over time, and it comes down over time, not in a single triumphant argument but in a long accumulation of small recognitions and a changed environment. This is slower than we want, and it is worth knowing in advance, so that you do not take the slowness as failure when the doubt is still speaking weeks or months after you first saw it for what it was.

When the doubt outlives the relationship

One of the most disorienting discoveries is that the doubt does not leave when the accuser does. People expect that once the relationship ends or the truth becomes clear, the self-blame will lift, and they are dismayed to find it still running long after, sometimes for years. If that is your situation, understand that you are not failing at recovery and the persistence is not evidence that the accusation was true after all. It is evidence of how deeply the voice was installed. Something built through years of repetition does not vanish because the circumstances changed; it has become a groove in your thinking, and grooves take time to wear smooth.

This matters because the persistence of the doubt can itself become a fresh accusation you level at yourself: I should be over this, the fact that I still feel like the abuser must mean I really am one. That reasoning is the installed voice finding a new disguise. The lingering of self-blame after harm is ordinary and expected, and it says nothing about your guilt. Solenne was troubled less by the original accusation than by the fact that it kept speaking in her own voice two years on, and what steadied her was learning that this was not a sign of hidden truth but a sign of deep installation, the predictable aftermath of having your reality rewritten for a long time. The voice speaking now is an echo of then, not a report from a reliable judge, and echoes, given a quieter room, grow fainter.

The self that was there before

There is one more piece of this worth naming, because it offers a way back. The installed voice tries to convince you that its account of you is the only account, that you have always been the selfish, toxic, or abusive person it describes. But you were yourself before this voice moved in, and the person you were then is evidence. Before the relationship that rewrote you, you had a sense of yourself, held by people who knew you, reflected in how you treated others across a whole life. That earlier self did not vanish; it was buried under the repetition, and part of recovery is remembering it.

This is why the people who knew you before matter so much, and why the reversal so often works to cut you off from them. They remember a version of you that predates the accusation, and their memory can serve as a counterweight to the installed voice until your own has recovered. Solenne found that a single old friend, one who had known her for twenty years and simply did not recognize the selfish monster she had come to believe she was, did more to loosen the voice than any amount of private reasoning. The friend was not arguing. She was remembering, out loud, a real person the accusation had tried to erase. That remembered self is not a fiction. It is the truth the voice was installed to bury, and it is still there to be reclaimed.

Trying it on your own situation

Begin to separate the installed voice from your own judgment, gently and over time.

First, write down the harshest thing the doubt says to you, in its exact words. Then ask whose voice that sentence is really in. Many readers recognize the precise phrasing of the person who harmed them, and seeing the sentence as a quotation rather than a truth is the beginning of setting it down.

Second, when the critical voice starts, practice naming it: that is the installed voice, not my judgment. You are not arguing with it or trying to defeat it. You are labeling it, which slowly strips it of its authority.

Third, keep a short record of moments when your perception turned out to be accurate, times you remembered rightly or read a situation correctly. You are rebuilding trust in an instrument that was deliberately undermined, and evidence of its reliability, gathered over time, is how that trust returns.

Fourth, when you catch the doubt punishing you for still feeling guilty long after the relationship ended, add a second label to it: that is not proof, that is an echo. Say it plainly. The doubt will try to use its own persistence as evidence against you, and naming that move for what it is, an echo rather than a report, takes away its newest weapon. You are allowed to still feel the old feelings and to know, at the same time, that feelings installed by harm are not testimony about your character.

A closing word of care, because this chapter sits close to the tender place where people turn on themselves. If the installed voice is loud enough that it is affecting your ability to function, your sleep, your work, your will to keep going, please treat that as a reason to reach for a qualified professional, not as one more failing to add to the list. The voice lies most convincingly when it tells you that you must handle it in isolation and that seeking help would only confirm your unworthiness. That is the installation protecting itself. You deserve support in quieting a voice that was never yours to begin with, and getting that support is one of the clearest acts of self-respect available to you.

What to carry forward

The doubt feels true because it was installed, placed in you through betrayal and repetition by someone who benefited from your self-blame. The mind tilts toward self-blame under betrayal because doubting yourself can feel safer than facing that a trusted person harmed you (Freyd, 1996), and gaslighting compounds this by wearing down the very perception you would need to judge the accusation (Sweet, 2019). Feeling like the abuser is not the same as being one, because the feeling was manufactured by these forces and does not track your actual conduct, which is why you rely on the method of the self-check rather than on the feeling. Name the installed voice as a quotation rather than a verdict, and rebuild trust in your perception through evidence over time. With the doubt loosened, the next chapter gives you the markers, direction, power, and fear, that let you read the true shape of what happened rather than the shape the accusation asserts.

Chapter 5: What a Pattern Reveals

Vaelan was handed a tidy phrase that nearly ended him: it takes two. He was forty-one, and when his relationship collapsed and he tried to describe what had happened to him, again and again he met the same response, from friends, from a counselor, even at first from himself. Relationships are complicated. There are two sides to every story. It takes two to make a conflict. The phrases sounded balanced and wise, and they left him with nowhere to stand, because they quietly insisted that whatever had been done to him, he must have done half of it. He could point to individual moments where he had behaved badly, and each moment seemed to confirm the phrase. What he could not yet do was step back far enough to see the shape of the whole, which told a different story than any single moment could.

This chapter gives you the tool Vaelan lacked: the ability to read a pattern rather than a pile of incidents. Almost any single moment in a difficult relationship is ambiguous, and can be spun to make either person look like the aggressor. The truth about who was harming whom does not live in the individual moments. It lives in the pattern across them, and specifically in three features of that pattern: direction, power, and fear. Learning to read those three things is what lets you answer the mutual abuse claim, resolve your own confusion, and see your situation as it actually was rather than as the accusation frames it.

Direction, power, and fear

The principle of this chapter is that direction, power, and fear reveal the pattern. Abuse is not defined by the presence of bad behavior, because bad behavior appears in almost every troubled relationship on both sides. Abuse is defined by a pattern of power and control running predominantly in one direction. So when you want to know the truth of a relationship, you do not tally up incidents as though keeping score in a game where each side's fouls cancel out. You look at the direction the control ran, at who held the power, and at who was afraid. These three features cut through the fog that individual incidents create, because they describe the structure of the relationship rather than its isolated moments.

This is the understanding that survives the phrase it takes two. Yes, both people in a conflict may behave badly at times. But behaving badly at times is not the same as holding another person under a pattern of control, and treating the two as equivalent is precisely the error the reversal wants you to make. Once you can see that abuse is a matter of pattern and direction rather than a matter of who has ever done anything wrong, the false symmetry dissolves, and you can begin to see the actual shape of what you lived through.

Why the single incident lies

It is worth understanding why individual incidents are so misleading, because the reversal lives on them. Any single moment can be extracted and framed to reverse the roles. The time you shouted becomes proof you were aggressive. The time you left the house becomes proof you were abandoning. The time you checked their phone, after months of being lied to, becomes proof you were controlling. Each incident, isolated from its cause and its context, can be made to say the opposite of what it meant, and a person practiced at the reversal will collect exactly these moments and present them as the case against you.

The defense against this is not to prove you never had a bad moment, which is impossible and which the reversal is counting on. The defense is to insist on the pattern, because the pattern is where the truth lives and the pattern is what the reversal cannot easily fake. One late-night phone check is ambiguous. A years-long pattern of one person monitoring, controlling, and frightening the other is not, and neither is the pattern of a person reacting, at intervals, inside that control. When you feel yourself being pulled into defending or explaining a single incident, that is the moment to step back and speak about the pattern instead, because the incident was chosen precisely because it looks bad in isolation.

Who controls the terms

Power in a relationship shows itself in who controls the terms: whose preferences generally prevail, whose moods set the emotional weather, who adapts to whom. In a relationship shaped by coercive control, one person's needs, rules, and reactions dominate, and the other organizes their behavior around managing that dominance (Stark, 2007). This is often invisible from the inside while it is happening, because the person adapting comes to experience their own constant accommodation as normal, even as love. It becomes visible when you step back and ask, across the whole relationship, whose world everyone was living in.

Ask yourself concrete questions. Whose anger did the household organize itself to avoid. Whose approval did you find yourself constantly seeking. Who could end a discussion by a change of mood, and who had to manage that mood to stay safe. Who was free to be themselves, and who was always adjusting. These questions reveal the direction of power, and the direction of power is one of the clearest signs of the direction of harm. Vaelan, asking them, saw that for years the entire emotional life of the relationship had been organized around his partner's moods, and that his own bad moments had almost all been attempts, clumsy and sometimes wrong, to survive that organization. The phrase it takes two had hidden this completely.

Who is afraid

Of the three features, fear is the most revealing, because it is the hardest to fake to yourself and the most direct signal of harm. Control produces fear in the controlled, and so the question of who was afraid of whom, asked across the span of the relationship, tends to settle what the incidents obscure. A person who monitored another's moods to stay safe, who felt relief when the other left, who chose words carefully to avoid an explosion, who flinched at a tone of voice, was living in fear, and fear of that kind runs in the direction of harm. Fear is not the same as anger, and this distinction matters, because the reversal often points to your anger as if it settled everything. Anger can be a reaction to fear; the frightened person, cornered long enough, sometimes turns and shouts. So do not let your own anger be read as proof you were the dangerous one. Ask instead the deeper question of who, underneath the anger, was afraid. That is the question the reversal least wants asked, which is one more reason to ask it.

Ask the question in both directions, truthfully. Were there moments the other person was afraid of you. If there were genuine ones, take them seriously and carry them to the repair chapter. But then ask the larger structural question: across the years, who lived in a state of watchfulness and fear, and who generated it. For most people this book is written for, the answer, once faced, is not the answer the accusation asserts. You were not the one others walked on eggshells around. You were the one walking. Naming that reverses the reversal, not by argument, but by looking at the plain structure of fear in the relationship you actually lived.

Reaching a fair reading, not a forced one

A caution belongs here, in keeping with the care this book takes throughout. The goal of reading the pattern is a fair reading, not a self-serving one. It is possible to misuse the language of direction, power, and fear, to insist that you were always the frightened one when the truth was more mixed. The check against this misuse is the same willingness the earlier chapters asked of you: to look at the genuine moments when you held power or generated fear, to own them where they were real, and still to weigh the overall direction truthfully. A fair reading can hold that you were, at times, part of the problem, and that the overall pattern of control and fear ran in one direction, and that direction was not yours. Most readers, looking fairly, will find exactly that. The point is not to win the argument that you were perfectly innocent, which no one is, but to see the true shape, which is almost always clearer and kinder to you than the accusation allowed.

When the pattern is genuinely mixed

Candor requires acknowledging that not every situation resolves into a clean single direction, and a book that promised otherwise would be lying to some of its readers. There are relationships in which both people held power at different times, both generated fear, both controlled and were controlled, and the pattern is genuinely mixed rather than one-directional. If that is your situation, reading the pattern will not hand you the comfort of pure victimhood, and you should not force it to. What it will give you is something more useful: an accurate map of a complicated reality, in which you can see the parts that were done to you and the parts that were yours, without collapsing either into the other.

A mixed pattern is not the same as the mutual abuse claim, and the difference matters. The mutual abuse claim is usually asserted to erase a one-directional pattern by declaring a false symmetry. A genuinely mixed pattern is something you discover by looking fairly, and it calls for a genuinely mixed response: owning your real share through the repair chapter, while still refusing any portion of the accusation that does not fit. Even in a mixed situation, the accusation that you are the abuser, the one, the origin, the pattern, is usually still false, because mixed is not the same as you being the perpetrator. Seeing your situation as genuinely mixed, where it is, is not a defeat. It is the accuracy this book values above comfort, and accuracy is what you can build a real recovery on.

Speaking the pattern to others

Reading the pattern for yourself is one thing; conveying it to others is another, and the two require different skills. When you try to explain a pattern of harm to someone who was not there, you face a real difficulty: patterns are cumulative and hard to convey quickly, while incidents are vivid and easy to grasp. This is part of why the reversal is so effective with an audience, because a single dramatic incident, your reaction, lands faster than a slow pattern of control. If you try to counter it by listing every incident on your side, you sound embattled and obsessive, which confirms the reversed picture.

The more effective approach, which later chapters develop, is to speak in terms of the overall shape rather than to relitigate every incident. Not a catalog of grievances, but a calm, brief description of the direction things ran: over the years, this was a relationship in which I was managing another person's moods and adapting to their control, and my worst moments were reactions inside that. You will not convince everyone, and you do not need to, but the people capable of hearing a pattern will hear it better in this form than buried under a hundred incidents. For now, the skill to build is seeing the pattern clearly yourself, because you cannot convey to anyone else a shape you have not yet made out for your own eyes.

Trying it on your own situation

Read your own pattern along the three features, patiently and on real material.

First, take five specific incidents that have been used against you, and for each one write what came before it and what it was responding to. Watch how differently they read with their context restored.

Second, answer the power questions in writing: whose moods set the weather, whose approval you sought, who adapted to whom across the relationship. Let the direction show itself across many examples rather than forcing a verdict from one.

Third, answer the fear question in both directions truthfully, and then write one sentence naming the overall direction of control and fear as you now see it. That sentence is the true shape of what happened, and it is the ground the mutual abuse claim cannot take from you.

Fourth, take the phrase that has been used to flatten your experience, whether it takes two, or you were both toxic, or there are two sides, and write underneath it the pattern you have now mapped. Set the tidy phrase against the actual shape. Many readers find that the phrase, which sounded so balanced and wise, simply does not survive contact with the direction, power, and fear they can now see plainly. The phrase was doing work: it was keeping a one-directional pattern hidden behind a mask of fairness. Naming that is how you take back the ground the phrase stole from you. Fairness that erases a real difference in harm is not fairness. It is the reversal wearing fairness as a disguise.

A closing reassurance. Reading the pattern can be a strange grief, because seeing the true shape often means accepting that a relationship you hoped was mutual was not, that you were more harmed than you let yourself know. That grief is real, and it is a sign of clarity, not of self-pity. You are not indulging yourself by naming the direction of harm accurately; you are recovering a truth that was deliberately obscured. Be gentle as you look, take it in pieces if the whole is too much, and lean on steady people or a professional as you go. The shape was always there. You are only now being allowed to see it, and seeing it, however sorrowful, is the ground everything else in this book is built on. A true map, even of hard terrain, is what you steer by. A false one, however comforting its symmetry, only keeps you lost.

Where this leaves you

The truth of who harmed whom does not live in individual incidents, which are ambiguous and easily reversed, but in the pattern across them, read through direction, power, and fear. Abuse is a pattern of power and control running predominantly in one direction, not a tally of bad moments that cancel out, which is why the phrase it takes two so badly misleads (Stark, 2007). The single incident lies because it can be stripped of context and framed to reverse the roles, and the defense is to insist on the pattern the reversal cannot fake. Power shows in who controls the terms, and fear, the most revealing feature, shows in who lived in watchfulness of whom. Read fairly rather than self-servingly, most readers find a single direction of harm that was not theirs. With the true shape in view, the book turns outward, to the painful reality that others often believe the reversed story, and how to stay steady when they do.

Chapter 6: When the Room Believes the Story

Orlian watched it happen in real time at a family dinner, and she said afterward it was like watching a magic trick she could see through but could not stop. She was forty, and her sister had been the one harming her for years, in the quiet, deniable ways that leave no marks. At the dinner, when Orlian finally raised something directly, her sister did not argue. She grew tearful, spoke softly about how hard she had tried, and wondered aloud, with wounded gentleness, why Orlian was always so angry with her. The room turned. Orlian could feel it turn. Within minutes she was the aggressor who had upset a family gathering, and her sister was the fragile, loving one under attack. Everyone at the table, people who loved Orlian, rearranged themselves around the reversed story, and Orlian sat there knowing the truth and watching it become invisible.

This chapter is about that turning of the room, the way the reversal persuades not just the accuser but the audience, so that friends, family, colleagues, and communities come to believe you are the problem. It is one of the loneliest parts of the whole experience, because the people you would turn to for support are often the very people being turned against you. Understanding why observers are swayed, and how to carry yourself when they are, is what this chapter offers. It will not promise that you can win the room back, because often you cannot, at least not quickly. It will show you why the room turned and how to keep your footing while it is turned.

Steady when disbelieved

The principle of this chapter is to stay steady when disbelieved. When the room turns, every instinct screams at you to fight for it, to correct the record, to make everyone see. That fight almost always makes things worse, because a person urgently insisting they are not the aggressor, in the moment right after a calm accuser has performed wounded gentleness, looks exactly like the aggressor the accuser described. The steadiness this chapter asks of you is not passivity and it is not surrender. It is the refusal to be provoked by the room's disbelief into the very behavior that confirms the reversal. You keep your footing not by winning the moment, but by declining to lose yourself in it.

This is hard because being disbelieved by your own people cuts deep, and the urge to be seen truly is one of the most human urges there is. But the moment right after the reversal has captured a room is the worst possible time to make your case, because the ground is tilted and anything you say rolls downhill into the reversed story. Steadiness buys you time, protects you from confirming the picture, and preserves your energy for the people and moments where being heard is actually possible. The room that turned quickly can turn back slowly, but only if you do not spend yourself trying to force it in the moment it is most against you.

Why observers are swayed

You will handle the turned room better if you understand that intelligent, caring people can be genuinely moved by the reversal, and that their being moved is not proof of anything about you. Research on this tactic has found that when people are exposed to the deny, attack, and reverse pattern, their perception of who is credible can shift toward the person using the tactic and against the target (Harsey & Freyd, 2020). The people at Orlian's table were not stupid or disloyal. They were human observers exposed to a practiced reversal, and the reversal did to their perception what it is designed to do.

Understand, too, that observers are at a structural disadvantage. They did not witness the private pattern of control; they see only this moment, in which one person is composed and wounded and the other is upset and accusing. They have no access to the years that produced the scene, only to its surface, and on the surface the reversal is convincing by design. This is why the calm performance of victimhood is so effective: it gives observers a simple, sympathetic story that fits what they can see, while the truth requires them to imagine a pattern they never witnessed. Their belief in the reversed story is a comment on the power of the tactic and the limits of their vantage, not a reliable judgment about your character.

The performance of victimhood

It helps to recognize the specific performance, so that it does not blindside you each time. The person running the reversal, faced with an audience, will often present as the reasonable, wounded, forgiving party. They may express sadness rather than anger, which reads as maturity. They may say generous-sounding things about you, which makes them appear fair and you appear harsh by contrast. They may wonder, softly, why you are so angry, which reframes your legitimate grievance as unprovoked aggression. None of this is spontaneous. It is the reversal tuned for an audience, and it is effective precisely because it does not look like a tactic. It looks like grace under attack.

Recognizing the performance protects you from two errors. The first is being so stunned by it that you freeze and let it stand unchallenged in your own mind, coming to doubt yourself because the performance was so convincing. The second, and more damaging, is reacting to it, letting your outrage at the performance pull you into exactly the heated behavior that confirms the story. The counter to the performance is not a better performance of your own, and it is certainly not visible anger at theirs. It is the quiet steadiness that does not give the audience the second act they are half-expecting, the moment where the accused proves the accusation by exploding.

When the group or institution turns

Sometimes it is not only a room but a whole community, congregation, workplace, or family system that accepts the reversed story, and when that happens the harm is compounded, because the group's authority lends weight to the reversal. Being disbelieved by an institution you relied on, or cast out by a community that was your support, is a distinct wound layered on top of the original one, and its pain is real and recognized (Smith & Freyd, 2014). If this has happened to you, the isolation can feel total, and the temptation to either rage at the whole group or collapse into believing them can be overwhelming.

Neither serves you. Raging at the group confirms the story to the very people you might otherwise slowly reach. Collapsing into their judgment hands the reversal a total victory it has not earned. The steadier path, developed in the next chapters, is to stop trying to move the whole group, to find and hold the few who can still see you, and to let your steady conduct over time speak where your protests cannot. Groups that turn quickly on a reversed story sometimes turn back as the fuller picture emerges, but that slow correction depends on your not having confirmed the story in the meantime by the way you responded to being disbelieved.

Why frantic defense confirms the story

It is worth understanding precisely why the natural response, urgent self-defense, backfires so reliably, because understanding it is what makes restraint possible. When you are accused and disbelieved, the story in the room is that you are the aggressive, unstable, difficult one. Every feature of frantic defense, the raised voice, the urgency, the flood of words, the visible distress, matches that story. The observers cannot see your innocence; they can only see your behavior, and agitated self-defense looks like agitation, which is what they were told to expect. You end up illustrating the accusation while trying to refute it.

There is also a asymmetry that makes this worse, which the earlier books in this series describe. Negative and dramatic impressions form fast and stick hard, faster and harder than calm, undramatic truth (Baumeister et al., 2001). A single heated outburst in front of a turned room can outweigh months of steady conduct, because the outburst is vivid and the steadiness is quiet. This is deeply unfair, and it is real, and knowing it is what lets you choose the harder, wiser path of not performing the distress the room is primed to read as guilt. Your calm is not only dignified; it is strategic, because it denies the story the vivid confirmation it is fishing for.

The relief of stopping the campaign

There is a particular exhaustion that comes from trying to correct a turned room, going from person to person, retelling your side, monitoring who believes you and who does not, and it is worth naming because putting it down is part of your recovery. Many people in your position spend months or years in this campaign, and it consumes them, because it is unwinnable in the form they are attempting. You cannot argue a whole social world back to the truth by force of repetition, and the effort keeps you tethered to the accusation, living inside it, unable to move on.

There is real relief on the other side of stopping. When you accept that you cannot control what the turned room believes, and that your energy is better spent on your own steadiness and on the few who can still see you, an enormous weight lifts. This is not giving up on the truth; it is giving up on a method that does not work. The truth has a longer timeline than a single confrontation, and it is often served better by your calm, consistent conduct over months than by any amount of urgent correction. Orlian stopped trying to win the family back at the next dinner, and the one after, and the exhaustion that had been eating her began to ease, not because the family suddenly saw clearly, but because she had stopped pouring herself into a fight she could not win on those terms. She turned her energy inward and toward the two relatives who had never turned, and that is where it began to do some good.

Time and the turned room

There is one more thing to hold about the turned room, and it is a genuine source of hope on a discouraging subject. A reversal performed for an audience is loudest and most convincing when it is new, and it requires constant maintenance to stay convincing. The accuser has to keep performing the wounded role, keep retelling the story, keep managing the impression, because it is not the truth and untrue things need continual upkeep. Your steadiness needs no such upkeep. You simply keep being who you are, and over months and years the people around you accumulate their own observations, which slowly rub against the reversed story.

This is why the long timeline favors you if you do not sabotage it. The relative who turned against Orlian at the dinner did not stay turned forever; over a couple of years, watching Orlian remain calm and decent while her sister's performances grew more strained, that relative quietly came back, saying only that she had started to see things differently. No argument had done it. Time and steady conduct had done it, working on an observer who was finally given enough of both to see past the performance. You cannot force this and you cannot schedule it, and it will not reach everyone. But it is real, and it means the turned room is not necessarily permanent. It is a snapshot taken at the tactic's strongest moment, and snapshots fade as the fuller picture develops.

Trying it on your own situation

Build the capacity to stay steady when you are not believed.

First, write down one time the room turned, and identify the performance that turned it: the tears, the soft wondering, the generous-seeming words. Naming the performance helps you see the turning as a tactic working rather than as the truth being recognized.

Second, prepare one calm, brief sentence for the moment you are disbelieved, something like: I see this differently, and I am not going to argue it here. Having it ready keeps you from either frantic self-defense or a wounded explosion.

Third, list the people, even one or two, who did not turn, who still see you. The next chapter is about them, and beginning the list now reminds you that the turned room is not the whole world.

Fourth, decide, deliberately, to step back from any campaign to correct the turned room, and write down what you will do with the energy instead. Perhaps you will put it toward your own steadiness, or toward the few who still see you, or toward rebuilding your life outside the reversed story. The point is to redirect the energy consciously rather than letting it keep bleeding into an unwinnable fight. You are not conceding that the story is true. You are declining to spend your one life trying to argue a tilted room level, and choosing instead to build on ground that is actually yours.

A closing word for the particular grief of this chapter, being disbelieved by your own people. It is one of the loneliest experiences a person can have, and there is no use pretending it does not cut to the bone. If the turned room includes people whose belief mattered to you most, family, old friends, a community that was your home, then you are grieving a real loss on top of the original harm, and that grief deserves room and support. Please do not carry it in isolation. The people who still see you, the subject of the next chapter, are part of how you survive this, and a good professional can help you hold the loss without letting it convince you that the reversed story was true. The room turned. That is a fact about the tactic and the limits of what others could see. It is not the verdict on you it appears to be.

What to carry forward

The reversal persuades not only the accuser but the audience, and the room that turns against you does so because intelligent observers exposed to the tactic have their perception genuinely shifted (Harsey & Freyd, 2020). Stay steady when disbelieved, because fighting for the room in the moment right after a wounded performance confirms the very picture painted of you. Observers are at a structural disadvantage, seeing only the composed accuser and the upset accused, not the years of private pattern, so their belief is a measure of the tactic's power, not of your character. Recognize the performance of victimhood and refuse to give it a second act, and where a whole group or institution turns, know the compounded wound is real (Smith & Freyd, 2014) while still declining to rage or collapse. Steadiness preserves you for the people and moments where being heard is possible, which begins with learning to answer the accusation itself, the subject of the next chapter.

Chapter 7: Answer the Charge, Not the Shame

Auren wrote a two thousand word message at two in the morning and, for once, did not send it. They were thirty-eight, and the accusation from their former partner had arrived by text, a long paragraph naming Auren as manipulative and abusive and cruel, and every cell in Auren's body wanted to answer it fully, to lay out the whole truth, to make the accuser finally understand. So they wrote it all, the entire history, every defense, every counter, two thousand words of it, and their thumb hovered over send. Then they remembered something from the earlier book in this series, and they stopped. They read their message back not as themselves but as a stranger would, and they saw it: it read like the ranting of exactly the unstable, obsessive person the accusation described. They deleted it and wrote, instead, one sentence. That one sentence protected them. The two thousand words would have hanged them.

This chapter is about how to respond to the accusation, and its central lesson is that the way you answer either confirms the reversed story or quietly refuses it. The instinct, when accused of something false and shameful, is to answer the shame: to defend your whole character, to prove you are not the monster, to make the accuser and everyone else understand the truth of who you are. That instinct, followed, almost always deepens the hole. This chapter teaches a different move: to answer the specific charge, calmly and narrowly, while refusing to be drawn into defending your soul, because your soul is not actually on trial in a way that frantic defense can win.

Answer the charge, not the shame

The principle is to answer the charge, not the shame. An accusation has two layers. There is the specific charge, the concrete claim that you did some particular thing, and there is the shame it invokes, the assault on your whole worth and character. Frantic responders answer the shame: they hear you are abusive and respond to the whole weight of that word, defending their entire self, which produces long, emotional, sprawling responses that confirm the picture of instability. Steady responders answer only the charge, narrowly and calmly, if it deserves an answer at all, and decline to perform a defense of their character, because performing that defense is what the reversal wants.

This distinction changes everything about how you respond. If the charge is a specific, factual claim that genuinely needs a response, you answer that claim, briefly and factually, and nothing more. If the accusation is mostly an attack on your character with no specific answerable claim, you may not need to respond at all. Either way, you refuse to take the bait of defending your worth, because your worth is not the kind of thing that can be established by argument in the middle of an accusation, and every attempt to establish it there makes you look more like the accused than less.

Why rage, groveling, and over-explaining all fail

There are three natural responses to being named the abuser, and it is worth seeing why each one fails, because you will feel the pull of all three. Rage feels justified, because the accusation is unjust, but rage confirms the story directly: an angry response to being called abusive looks like abusiveness to anyone watching, and it hands the accuser exactly the reaction they can point to. Groveling, the opposite response, feels like it might buy peace, but excessive apology and self-abasement read as an admission, and they invite the accuser to pile on more, because you have signaled that the accusation is landing. Over-explaining, the most common response among thoughtful people, feels like the reasonable path, but a flood of explanation reads as defensiveness and obsession, and it gives the accuser endless material to twist.

What these three have in common is that they all answer the shame rather than the charge, and they all give the reversal what it wants: a reaction, a confirmation, more material. The steady alternative is narrow and calm, and it feels deeply unsatisfying, because it does not discharge the enormous emotional pressure the accusation creates. That is precisely why it works. The pressure to rage, grovel, or explain is the pressure the tactic is counting on, and declining to discharge it in your response is how you keep your footing. You handle the emotional pressure elsewhere, with support and in private, so that it does not leak into the response where it would be used against you.

The narrow, calm answer

What does answering the charge actually look like. It is brief, it is factual, and it is unemotional, in the way you learned in the companion volumes as writing for a third reader. If there is a specific claim that needs correcting, you correct it in a sentence or two, without heat and without a counter-attack. That did not happen; here is what did, briefly. Or: I disagree with that characterization, and I am not going to argue it. Or, often best, nothing whatever, because a false accusation that consists only of character attack frequently deserves silence, and silence leaves the accusation sitting by itself, unamplified by your reaction. Each of these forms shares the same discipline: you decide, before you feel the pull to defend, that your response will be no larger than the specific answerable claim, and that everything beyond that claim, the character attack, the invitation to fight, the bid for your collapse, will go unanswered. The size of your response is itself a message. A brief, factual reply to a sprawling accusation says, without a word of argument, that you do not accept the frame, that you will address what is real and decline the rest, and that your composure is not available for the taking.

The power of the narrow answer is that it gives the reversal nothing to work with. There is no rage to point to, no groveling admission to exploit, no sprawling explanation to twist. There is only a calm, brief, factual person declining to perform the role they have been assigned. To any third party who reads it later, and in these situations there is often a later reader, the narrow answer reads as the communication of a reasonable person, while the accuser's long emotional attack reads as what it is. Auren's one sentence, set against their former partner's paragraph of accusation, told a truer story to anyone who saw the exchange than two thousand words of defense ever could have.

What never to put in your answer

Some things should stay out of any response, no matter how strong the pull, because they will be used against you. Never match the accuser's cruelty, because your matching cruelty is what survives in the record while their provocation fades. Never counter-accuse in the same breath as you defend, because it reads as deflection and escalation. Never make threats of any kind, even ones that feel like justice. Never write in the heat of the first reaction; the delay you learned in the companion volumes, waiting until your body has settled before you respond to anything that stings, prevents most of the responses you would regret. And never try, in the response itself, to make the accuser understand or admit the truth, because that is the one thing the response cannot achieve, and reaching for it is what produces the two thousand words.

That last point deserves emphasis, because it is the hook that catches thoughtful people. You want the accuser to understand. You want them to see what they have done, to acknowledge the truth, to release you from the false story. The response to the accusation is not where that happens, and it is almost never going to happen at all, because the accuser is running a tactic, not making a mistake they would correct if they only understood. Letting go of the hope of being understood by the accuser is what frees you to write the narrow, calm answer instead of the sprawling, desperate one.

When silence is the whole answer

It deserves its own treatment, because thoughtful people struggle with it most: a great many accusations are best met with no response at all. When an accusation contains no specific, answerable claim, when it is purely an attack on your character, purely a wounded performance, purely bait, then there is nothing there to answer, and answering it only feeds it. Silence in that situation is not weakness and it is not a concession. It is the recognition that the accusation was not a question seeking a truthful reply but a move seeking a reaction, and you are declining to supply the reaction.

This is hard because silence in the face of a false accusation feels unbearable, as though not answering were the same as agreeing. It is not. To any later observer, an unanswered attack often reads as an attack that did not warrant a response, while a frantic reply reads as a nerve struck. And to you, the practice of not answering is a way of taking back a piece of your life, because every accusation you do not answer is time and energy you keep for yourself instead of pouring it into the tactic. Auren learned, over months, that most of what arrived required nothing from them, and that the silence they had feared would look like guilt actually looked, to everyone including themselves, like a person who had stopped playing a game they could not win.

Handle the pressure somewhere else

The narrow answer only works if you have somewhere to put the enormous emotional pressure that the accusation creates, because that pressure is real and it has to go somewhere. If you swallow it entirely and let it build, it will eventually burst out, often in exactly the rage or flood the tactic is fishing for. So the discipline of the calm response is not about suppressing what you feel; it is about routing it away from the response and toward a place where it can be safely discharged. You write the two thousand words, and you do not send them; you say them to a trusted friend, or a therapist, or a page in a private notebook, where they harm no one and give the reversal nothing.

This is why the people who manage the narrow answer are not the ones with superhuman composure, but the ones with somewhere to take their pain. The rage at the injustice, the desperate wish to be understood, the grief of being named the abuser, all of it is valid and all of it needs expression, just not in the reply to the accuser. When Auren stopped trying to discharge their pain into the response and started bringing it to a friend and a journal instead, the narrow answer stopped feeling like suppression and started feeling like strategy. The feeling was fully honored; it was simply honored in a place where it could do some good rather than in the one place it would be used against them. Protect the response by giving the feeling a better home. A useful image is a pressure valve: the accusation raises the pressure, and if the only outlet is the reply to the accuser, the reply will blow. Build other outlets, deliberately and in advance, so that by the time you compose any response the pressure has already been released elsewhere and the reply can be as narrow and cool as the situation calls for. The people who do this well are not less angry than everyone else; they simply have more places to put the anger, and so none of it has to come out in the one place that would be used against them.

Trying it on your own situation

Practice the narrow answer on a real accusation, in writing, before you need it.

First, take an accusation you have received and separate the charge from the shame: underline any specific, answerable claim, and set aside the character attack. Notice how little of the accusation is actually a specific claim, and how much is an assault on your worth.

Second, draft two responses: the full one you want to send, defending everything, and the narrow one that answers only a specific claim or says nothing. Read both as a stranger would, and see which one protects you.

Third, write your own rule for responding to accusations, in advance and in a calm moment: I will wait before responding, answer only specific claims briefly, decline to defend my character, and take my pain elsewhere. A rule set in advance is far easier to keep than a decision made in the heat of an accusation.

Fourth, name in advance where your pain will go when an accusation lands, so the narrow answer has somewhere to route the pressure. Write down the person you will call, the notebook you will open, or the practice you will use to discharge what you feel, before you touch the reply. Deciding this ahead of time is what makes the calm response survivable, because you will not be asking yourself to simply swallow an unbearable feeling; you will be moving it, deliberately, to a place it can be safely felt. The response stays narrow because the feeling has a better home.

A closing word on dignity, because that is what this chapter is really about. Answering the charge and not the shame can feel, at first, like letting the accusation stand, like failing to defend your own name. It is the opposite. Refusing to perform the role you were assigned, declining to rage or grovel or flood, keeping your reply calm and your pain in its proper place, is the most dignified thing you can do in the face of a false accusation, and dignity, unlike frantic defense, is legible to everyone watching over time. You do not restore your name by fighting for it in the accuser's arena on the accuser's terms. You restore it by being, steadily and unmistakably, a person whose conduct does not match the story, until the gap between the two becomes the most visible thing about the whole affair.

Where this leaves you

The way you answer an accusation either confirms the reversed story or quietly refuses it, and the key is to answer the charge, not the shame. An accusation has two layers, the specific answerable claim and the assault on your whole worth, and frantic responders defend their worth, which produces the rage, groveling, or over-explaining that all confirm the picture. The steady answer is narrow, calm, factual, and often silent, giving the reversal no reaction to exploit and reading, to any later observer, as the voice of a reasonable person (Harsey & Freyd, 2020; Baumeister et al., 2001). Keep cruelty, counter-accusation, threats, and the hope of being understood out of your response, and handle the emotional pressure elsewhere. Responding well to the words is one thing; dealing with the person who keeps sending them is another, and the next chapter turns to facing the accuser directly, and to when the wisest response is distance.

Chapter 8: Facing the Accuser

Évren spent three years trying to be understood by the one person who would never understand him, and the day he stopped was the day he began to recover. He was forty-four, and long after the relationship ended, he was still, in his head and sometimes in person, arguing his case to his former partner. He would compose explanations. He would seize on a civil exchange as a chance to finally make her see. He would replay their conversations, searching for the words that would have unlocked her understanding. All of it kept him tethered to her, living in her judgment, organizing his inner life around a verdict she was never going to give. What freed him was a single grim realization: she was not withholding understanding by accident, and no sentence he could ever construct would produce it, because the misunderstanding was not a mistake. It was the tactic.

This chapter is about facing the accuser directly, the person who named you, and about the hardest thing to give up in this whole ordeal: the hope of being understood by them. It is also about the practical business of dealing with someone who may still be in your life, through shared children, shared work, shared family, or shared history, and about the times when the right and safe response is distance. Facing the accuser well begins with releasing a hope, and that release, painful as it is, is one of the most freeing moves available to you.

You do not owe the argument

The principle of this chapter is that you do not owe the accuser the argument. Something in you insists that you must make them understand, that you cannot rest until they acknowledge the truth, that their false view of you is an open wound that only their correction can close. This insistence is natural, and it is a trap, because it places the key to your peace in the hands of the one person guaranteed not to turn it. The accuser is running a reversal, which means their misunderstanding of you is not a gap to be filled with better explanation but a position they are maintaining on purpose. You do not owe them the argument, you will not win it, and every round you play keeps you captive.

Releasing the argument does not mean you accept the accusation or concede the point. It means you stop trying to change the mind of someone committed to misjudging you, and you redirect that enormous energy toward the things that can actually heal: your own clarity, your recovery, the few who can see you. This is not giving up. It is giving up on a method that does not work and cannot work, and reclaiming the effort you have been pouring into it. The argument with the accuser is the black hole of this whole experience, and stepping back from its edge is how you keep from being pulled apart.

Why understanding will not come

It is worth being clear about why the understanding you long for will not arrive, because the hope is stubborn and keeps regrowing unless you pull it up by the root. To understand you, in the way you want, the accuser would have to acknowledge that they harmed you and that their accusation reversed the truth. That acknowledgment is the exact thing the reversal is built to prevent. The whole tactic is a defense against accountability, and granting you understanding would mean surrendering that defense. Asking the accuser to understand you is therefore asking them to abandon the very strategy that is protecting them from their own conduct, which they are structurally unwilling to do (Freyd, 1997).

This is why your best explanations bounce off, why the conversation that should have worked did not, why you keep feeling that if you could just find the right words, they would finally see. There are no right words, because the problem was never that they lacked the words. They lack the willingness, and no eloquence of yours can supply a willingness they are determined not to have. Seeing this clearly is a grief, because it means giving up a hope you may have carried for years. It is also a liberation, because it releases you from a task that was never possible and that was consuming your life.

Limiting the contact you can limit

Where the accuser remains in your life, the practical work is to reduce and structure contact to what is genuinely necessary, so that the reversal has less surface to work on. If contact can end entirely, and it is safe for it to do so, that is often the cleanest path. Where it cannot, because of shared children or unavoidable ties, the companion volume on co-parenting develops the structured, low-contact approach in detail, and its core applies here: keep necessary communication brief, factual, and unemotional, move it onto channels that create a record, and refuse the bait of provocation. You are not trying to have a relationship with the accuser. You are trying to exchange only what must be exchanged, in a form that gives the tactic nothing.

The aim of all this structure is to shrink the accuser's presence in your life down to the smallest footprint the situation allows. Every unnecessary contact is an opening for a fresh provocation or a new accusation; every one you close is an opening denied. This is not pettiness or coldness. It is the removal of the surfaces the reversal needs, and it is one of the most protective things you can do, both for your safety and for your recovery, because you cannot heal while the source of the harm has constant access to you.

When distance is the right and safe choice

Sometimes the wisest and safest response is distance, up to and including ending contact entirely, and this chapter gives you permission to consider it without guilt. If a person is running a sustained reversal against you, continued contact often means continued harm, and there is no obligation to keep offering yourself to it in the name of maturity, closure, or hope. Distance is not an admission of guilt, whatever the accuser claims, and it is not a failure of character. It is a reasonable response to an unreasonable and ongoing harm.

Where there is any concern for your physical safety, this moves beyond the scope of a book, and you should treat it accordingly. If you fear for your safety or your children's, contact a qualified professional, a domestic abuse service, or the appropriate authorities in your area, because a book can offer understanding but it cannot offer protection, and protection is what safety requires. Within the range of situations this book addresses, the principle holds: you are allowed to protect yourself with distance, you do not need the accuser's permission or agreement to do so, and choosing distance from someone who keeps harming you is an act of self-respect, not a confirmation of anything they have said.

Refusing the renewed provocation

An accuser who remains in your life will often test the distance you set, and it helps to expect this so it does not catch you off guard. When you stop supplying the argument and reduce contact, the accuser frequently escalates for a time, sending sharper accusations, or switching suddenly to warmth and reasonableness to draw you back into engagement, or manufacturing a crisis that seems to demand your involvement. This renewed provocation is not a sign that your distance is wrong. It is a sign that the distance is working, because it is disrupting a dynamic that depended on your engagement, and the accuser is trying to restore it.

The task is to hold steady through the testing without either punishing or explaining. You do not announce your boundaries, justify them, or debate them, because announcements and justifications reopen the very engagement you are closing. You simply enact them: you answer only what genuinely must be answered, in the narrow calm form of the previous chapter, and you let the rest pass. Évren found that when he stopped responding to the provocations and stopped seizing on the warm moments as openings, the contact from his former partner intensified for a couple of months and then, gradually, thinned, because the surfaces it had been using were no longer there. Boundaries held quietly and without drama outlast the pressure against them, and the pressure, however sharp at first, tends to fade when it stops producing a response.

The grief of releasing the hope

It would be untruthful to present the release of the argument as purely freeing, because it is also a genuine loss that deserves to be mourned. To give up the hope that the accuser will one day understand is to give up a particular future you may have held onto for years: the conversation where they finally see, the acknowledgment that lifts the false story, the closure that lets you both move on with the truth restored. That future is not coming, and letting go of it is a real grief, the grief of a resolution you wanted and will not receive.

Let yourself feel that loss rather than rushing past it, because a grief denied tends to pull you back into the argument, seeking through renewed effort the closure you could not bear to mourn. The closure you were waiting for from the accuser is not available, but there is another kind of closure that is: the closure you give yourself, by reaching your own clear conclusion, releasing the impossible hope, and turning toward your life. It is a quieter closure than the one you wanted, and it does not require the accuser's participation, which is exactly what makes it reliable. Évren never got the conversation he had rehearsed for three years. What he got instead was the day he stopped needing it, and that day, unspectacular as it was, turned out to be the one that set him free.

Closure without the other person

Because the hope of being understood dies so hard, it is worth naming directly the alternative it makes room for. Most people imagine closure as something that happens between two people: an acknowledgment, an apology, a shared recognition of what was true. That kind of closure is lovely when it is available, and it is simply not available here, because the other person is committed to the reversal. If you make your peace conditional on their participation, you hand them permanent power over whether you ever heal.

The closure that is available is one you author on your own. It is made of the conclusion you reached in the self-check, the true shape you mapped of the pattern, the release of the impossible argument, and the deliberate turn toward a life the accuser does not run. None of these requires the accuser to do or say anything. They are entirely within your reach, which is exactly why they can be relied on. This is a demotion of the accuser from the center of your story to its edge, accomplished not by winning against them but by no longer needing anything from them. Évren described the moment he understood this as the first time in three years the accuser had grown smaller in his mind, not because she had changed, but because he had stopped enlarging her by waiting on her. The closure he had been seeking from her, he finally gave to himself, and it held, because it was the one kind of closure that did not depend on a person determined never to grant it. It was, in the end, the only closure that had ever truly been on offer, and recognizing that was itself a kind of release.

Trying it on your own situation

Move toward releasing the argument and structuring the contact.

First, write down the sentence you keep wishing the accuser would say, the understanding you are waiting for. Then write beside it: this will not come, because giving it would mean surrendering the tactic. Naming the impossibility is how you begin to release the hope.

Second, if the accuser remains in your life, choose one point of contact to reduce or structure this month, and decide the channel and the limits in advance, in a calm moment.

Third, ask yourself plainly whether more distance, or ending contact, would serve your safety and recovery, and if the truthful answer touches on your physical safety at all, identify now the professional or service you would contact. Deciding in advance means help is within reach if you need it.

Fourth, prepare for the testing before it comes. Write down, in advance, how you will respond when the accuser escalates or suddenly turns warm to draw you back: I will answer only what genuinely must be answered, in a brief and calm form, and let the rest pass. Deciding this in a settled moment is what carries you through the first weeks of a new distance, which are always the hardest, because a plan made in advance does not have to be invented under pressure. The testing is not a reason to abandon the distance. It is confirmation that the distance is doing its work.

A closing word on the loss at the center of this chapter. Giving up the hope of being understood by the person who harmed you is one of the heaviest things this book asks, and it is right to grieve it. But consider what you are trading it for. In place of a resolution that depends entirely on someone committed to withholding it, you gain a resolution that depends only on you: your own clarity, your own conclusion, your own turning toward a life the accuser no longer governs. That is a smaller closure than the one you dreamed of, and it is an incomparably more reliable one, because no one else holds the key to it. You waited a long time for them to set you free. It turns out you can do it yourself, and that is the only version that was ever truly available.

What to carry forward

You do not owe the accuser the argument, because their misunderstanding of you is not a gap to be filled with better explanation but a position they maintain on purpose, and the understanding you long for will not come, since granting it would mean surrendering the reversal that protects them from accountability (Freyd, 1997). Releasing that hope is a grief and a liberation, freeing the energy you have poured into an impossible task. Where the accuser remains in your life, reduce and structure contact to the smallest necessary footprint, and where distance or ending contact would serve your safety and recovery, you are permitted to choose it without guilt, turning to qualified help and the appropriate authorities wherever your physical safety is in question. With the accuser's presence shrunk and the argument released, the next chapter turns to the people who still see you truly, and how to keep and tend them.

Chapter 9: The Few Who Still See You

Éloane made a list one night of everyone who had fallen away, and it was long enough to frighten her. She was thirty-six, and in the year since the accusation began circulating, she had watched her social world thin out like a tide going out. Friends who used to call had gone quiet. A couple she and her former partner had been close to had chosen the former partner. Even some family had grown cool, repeating things they had heard as though they were established fact. Staring at the list of the lost, Éloane felt the full weight of the isolation the reversal had produced, and she nearly missed the thing that mattered more, which was the much shorter list on the other side of the page: the three people who had not fallen away, who still, without fuss, saw her.

This chapter is about those three people, and about the truth that you do not need the whole world to see you truly, you need a few who do. The reversal isolates, deliberately, because an isolated person is easier to overwhelm and easier to doubt. The counter to that isolation is not to win back the crowd, which is usually impossible and always exhausting, but to find, keep, and tend the few who never stopped seeing you. Those few are worth more than the crowd ever was, and building your recovery around them rather than around the people you lost is one of the wisest moves available to you.

The few who know you

The principle of this chapter is that a few who know you outweigh a crowd that turned. When the reversal spreads and your social world thins, the natural focus is on the loss, on all the people who believed the story and fell away. That focus, though understandable, keeps you oriented toward what you cannot control and cannot easily recover. The wiser orientation is toward the few who remained, because they are the ones who can actually sustain you, reflect your real character back to you, and hold the truth of who you are while your own hold on it recovers. A small number of solid people is not a consolation prize for the crowd you lost. It is the actual thing you need.

This reframing matters practically, because your energy is finite and a long recovery will demand most of it. Spent trying to win back a turned crowd, that energy mostly evaporates. Invested in the few who see you, it compounds, deepening the relationships that are keeping you standing. The reversal wants you isolated, and it half-succeeds when it takes the crowd; it fully succeeds only if, in mourning the crowd, you neglect the few. Turning deliberately toward those few is how you deny the reversal its complete victory, and it is how you rebuild a base of support that the tactic cannot easily reach.

Why isolation is the point

Understanding that the isolation is deliberate, not incidental, will change how you respond to it. The reversal seeks an audience and spreads the reversed story partly to build a chorus that reinforces itself, and partly to strip you of support, because a person cut off from their people is easier to control, easier to overwhelm, and easier to convince of their own guilt. Isolation is not a sad side effect of the accusation; it is one of its functions. Recovery and resilience depend heavily on connection, and a person deprived of support is far more vulnerable to being broken down (Herman, 1992). The tactic knows this without needing the research, and it works to cut you off precisely because your isolation serves it.

Seeing the isolation as a feature rather than a verdict changes its meaning. Each friend who fell away is not necessarily delivering a judgment on your character; many are simply people who heard one confident story, had no other information, and did what people do, which is believe the account in front of them. That is a disappointing fact about human beings, and it is usually not the malice or the moral verdict it feels like. Reframing the lost friendships this way does not remove the pain, but it removes the extra layer of self-condemnation, the sense that so many people falling away must mean the accusation was true. It does not mean that. It means the tactic did what it was built to do, and it did it to your relationships, not because of your guilt.

Tending the few

The few who remain need tending, not because they are fragile, but because relationships that sustain you through a long ordeal deserve care and attention rather than being taken for granted. This means reaching out to them, and not only when you are in crisis and need something, but simply to stay connected, to keep the relationship alive as a relationship and not only as a support line. It means, where you can, being truthful with them about what you are going through without making every interaction about the accusation, so that the friendship remains a place of ordinary human connection and not only a war room. And it means receiving their view of you, letting their steady sight of your real character be a counterweight to the installed voice, rather than deflecting it because you cannot yet believe it.

There is particular value in the people who knew you before the accusation, because they hold a memory of you that predates the reversal and cannot be overwritten by it. When the installed voice insists you have always been the monster the accusation describes, a friend who has known you for decades and simply does not recognize that description is offering evidence, not just comfort. Éloane found that one of her three, a friend of twenty years, did more to steady her than any reasoning she could do on her own, because the friend was not arguing that Éloane was good; she was simply remembering, without effort, the person she had always known, and that remembering reached past the installed voice to the self underneath it.

Answering the wider circle without frenzy

Beyond the few who see you and the crowd that turned, there is a wider circle of acquaintances who have heard something and are uncertain, and how you handle them matters, though not in the way you might think. The temptation is to launch a campaign of correction, to reach each uncertain person and set them straight. Resist it, for the reasons the earlier chapter gave: the campaign is exhausting, unwinnable in that form, and prone to making you look like the embattled aggressor the story describes. A useful test before you reach for anyone in this circle is to ask whether the contact is for their clarity or for your relief. If it is really about discharging your own distress, that distress has better homes, and reaching for an acquaintance to carry it usually backfires. The better approach with the wider circle is the calm, brief, non-defensive posture you have been learning, and then time. To someone who raises the accusation, a simple, steady line, that the situation is painful and you are not going to get into it, accomplishes more than an hour of defense.

The wider circle, like the turned room, tends to correct itself slowly as your steady conduct accumulates against a story that requires constant retelling to survive. You do not need to convert the uncertain by argument; you need to be, over time, visibly a person whose life and character do not match the accusation. Some of the wider circle will drift back toward accuracy on their own, some will not, and none of it requires the frantic effort the tactic would love to provoke. Your job with the wider circle is not to win it but to remain steady within it, and to keep your real energy for the few who never needed convincing.

When even the few are hard to trust

There is a complication worth naming, because it catches many people in your position: after being harmed by someone you trusted, and then disbelieved by people you counted on, trusting anyone can feel dangerous, even the few who never turned. The betrayal and the desertion together can leave you scanning even your loyal friends for signs that they, too, will eventually believe the story and fall away. This wariness is understandable, a natural bruise left by what happened, but if it is not recognized it can push away the very people who are trying to stay.

Go gently with yourself here, and go gently with them. You do not have to trust all at once, and you do not have to explain the wariness away. It is enough to notice it, to name it inwardly as a bruise rather than a truth about these particular people, and to let the few earn your trust slowly through their steadiness, which they generally will if you give them the chance. The reversal damaged your capacity to trust along with everything else, and part of recovery is letting safe people be safe again, at whatever pace you can manage. If the wariness is severe enough that it is isolating you further, that is worth raising with a professional, because relearning trust after this kind of harm is often more than willpower can accomplish on its own, and there is no shame in getting help with it.

Connection as a form of resistance

It helps to see that keeping and tending the few is not merely self-care but a form of quiet resistance to the tactic. The reversal wants you isolated, doubting, and cut off from any reflection of your real self. Every real connection you maintain works directly against that aim: it keeps a true mirror in your life, it keeps you from the total isolation the tactic seeks, and it reminds you, through ordinary human contact, that you are a person who is known and valued, not the figure the accusation describes. When you reach out to a loyal friend, you are not only comforting yourself; you are refusing the isolation the reversal is trying to impose.

This reframing can help on the days when reaching out feels like too much, when the shame whispers that you should withdraw and spare people the burden of you. That whisper is the tactic's voice, because your withdrawal serves it. Choosing connection anyway, even in a small way, even when you do not feel worthy of it, is a move against the reversal and toward your recovery. Éloane came to treat her weekly contact with her three as something close to a discipline, not because the friendships were work, but because on her worst days the isolating voice was loudest, and reaching out anyway was how she proved the voice wrong. The connection was the counter-argument, made not in words but in the simple fact of remaining in contact with people who saw her truly. There is a further quiet benefit worth naming: the few who see you can also, gently, correct your own distorted sight. When the installed voice has convinced you that you are the monster the accusation describes, a trusted friend who simply does not treat you as one is offering a steady counter-reading of you, day after day, that slowly erodes the distortion. You do not have to argue with them about it; you only have to let their ordinary, unremarkable regard for you register, and register again, until it begins to compete with the accusation on equal terms. That is another reason the few are worth tending: they are not only support, they are witnesses, and their witness is part of how you find your way back to an accurate view of yourself.

Trying it on your own situation

Turn your attention deliberately toward the people who still see you.

First, make the two lists Éloane made, but linger on the shorter one. Name the few, even one or two, who did not turn, who still see your real character. These are the people this chapter is about.

Second, reach out to one of them this week, not in crisis and not to discuss the accusation, but simply to stay connected as friends. Tending the relationship is the practice.

Third, prepare one calm line for anyone in the wider circle who raises the accusation, something like: it has been a painful situation and I would rather not get into it, but thank you for asking me directly. Having it ready keeps you steady where you would otherwise be pulled into frantic defense.

Fourth, when you notice yourself pulling away from a loyal friend out of shame or wariness, do the small opposite thing anyway: send the message, make the call, accept the invitation. You do not have to feel worthy of the connection to choose it, and choosing it is itself a move against the isolation the tactic wants. Treat contact with your few, on the hard days especially, as a quiet discipline rather than something to be earned by feeling good enough for it. The withdrawal is the reversal's voice; the reaching out is yours.

A closing word about grief and gratitude held together. This chapter asks you to mourn the people who fell away and to treasure the few who did not, and both are appropriate at once. The losses are real, and some of them will ache for a long time, and you are allowed to grieve friendships and family ties that the reversal cost you. At the same time, the few who stayed are a genuine gift, and orienting toward them rather than toward the losses is not denial; it is the choice to build your recovery on solid ground rather than on the sand of who you cannot get back. You lost more than you should have. You also kept more than the tactic wanted you to keep, and that keeping, tended well, is enough to rebuild on.

Where this leaves you

You do not need the whole world to see you truly; you need a few who do, and a small number of solid people outweighs the crowd that turned. The reversal isolates on purpose, because a person cut off from support is easier to overwhelm and easier to convince of their own guilt (Herman, 1992), which means each lost friendship is usually the tactic working rather than a verdict on your character.

Turn your finite energy toward tending the few who remained, especially those who knew you before and hold a memory the accusation cannot overwrite, and meet the wider circle with calm brevity and time rather than a frantic campaign. The few who see you are part of how you survive, and they are also part of how you rebuild, which brings us to the inner work of regulation and, after it, the recovery of your own sight, beginning with the discipline of not performing the very role the accusation predicts.

Chapter 10: Do Not Perform the Part

Alaris knew the exact message that would undo him, and so, eventually, did the person sending them. He was forty-two, and his former partner had learned, over years, precisely which words would break through his composure and produce the explosion she could then display as proof of his temper. A particular phrase about his parenting. A particular tone of mock concern. A particular accusation timed for the moment he was most tired. She would send it, and something in him would detonate, and within the hour a screenshot of his furious reply would be circulating as evidence of the very thing he was being accused of. Alaris was not an angry man. He was a tired, harmed man being played like an instrument, and the instrument always produced the same note, because he had never learned to keep his hand off the string.

This chapter is about that string, and about learning to keep your hand off it. The reversal does not only wait for your reactions; it fishes for them, deliberately, because your reaction is the evidence it needs and the confirmation it seeks. The single most protective skill you can build, therefore, is the ability to not perform the part, to receive the provocation without producing the explosion it is designed to trigger. This is not about suppressing your feelings, which does not work and is not healthy. It is about regulating your body so that the provocation does not automatically become the reaction, and that regulation, unlike willpower, can actually be learned.

Do not perform the part

The principle of this chapter is not to perform the part they have written for you. The accusation predicts that you are unstable, aggressive, and dangerous, and the reversal works to make that prediction come true by provoking exactly the behavior it describes.

Every time you supply the explosion, you complete the accusation for them; every time you receive the provocation without performing the predicted reaction, you break the mechanism the tactic depends on. This is not about being fake or emotionless. It is about refusing to be the puppet whose strings the accuser has learned to pull, and reclaiming the space between what is done to you and what you do in return.

Refusing to perform the part is powerful precisely because the part is what the reversal needs. A calm accuser and a raging accused is the picture that makes the reversal work; deny it the raging accused and the picture falls apart. This does not mean you never feel rage, which would be neither possible nor healthy. It means the rage does not automatically become the visible, recorded, displayable explosion the tactic is fishing for. You feel it, and you handle it, and you do not perform it on cue. That gap, between feeling and performing, is the whole of this chapter, and it is buildable.

Why willpower is not enough

You have probably already tried to simply decide not to react, and found that it fails at the crucial moment, and it is important to understand why, so you stop blaming your character for it. Provocation does not work primarily on your reasoning mind; it works on your body and nervous system, faster than thought. A well-aimed provocation triggers a threat response, a surge of activation that prepares the body to fight or flee, and this response fires before your deliberate, reasoning self has even fully registered what is happening. By the time you are consciously deciding to stay calm, your body is already activated, and willpower applied to an already-activated system is usually too little, too late (Porges, 2011).

This is why the failure to stay calm is not a moral failure. It is a physiological reality: a nervous system pushed into threat cannot be reliably overridden by good intentions. And it is why the solution is not more willpower but a different approach, one that works with the body rather than against it. Trauma and sustained harm make this even more pronounced, because a system that has been kept in threat for a long time becomes primed to react, quicker to fire and slower to settle (van der Kolk, 2014). If you have been reacting in ways that shame you, this is likely why, and the shame is misplaced. You were not weak. You were an activated system being deliberately activated, without the tools to work with your own physiology. Those tools are what this chapter provides.

The strategic pause

The core tool is the pause, and it is deceptively simple: you do not respond to provocation while activated, ever, as an absolute rule. This one rule, held without exception, does more than any amount of trying to feel calm, because it does not ask you to control the feeling, only to delay the action until the feeling has passed. When a provocation lands and you feel the surge, the surge is the signal, not to respond, but to wait, because the activated state passes if you let it, usually within twenty minutes or so if you stop feeding it. During the pause you do not compose the reply, do not rehearse the argument, do not stew, all of which keep the activation high. You do something that settles the body: slow breathing, especially a longer exhale than inhale, which speaks directly to the nervous system in a language it understands and signals that the threat has passed (Porges, 2011). You walk. You put the phone down and leave the room. You wait for the wave to crest and fall, and only then, from a settled state, do you decide whether and how to respond at all.

The pause works because it inserts time and physiology between the provocation and the response, exactly where the reversal wants no gap at all. The tactic depends on the immediacy of your reaction, on the string producing the note the instant it is plucked. The pause breaks the immediacy. It does not require you to be calmer by force in the moment of activation, which is nearly impossible; it requires only that you not act while activated, which is achievable, because not acting is easier than acting calmly. Alaris made one rule, the rule that eventually freed him: he would never reply to his former partner while his heart was pounding. He would feel the surge, recognize it as the signal to wait, and put the phone in a drawer until his body had settled, sometimes an hour, sometimes a day. The messages designed to detonate him stopped detonating him, not because he had become a calmer man, but because he had stopped letting the provocation reach the reply before his body had settled.

Knowing your own strings

Part of not performing the part is knowing which provocations are aimed at you specifically, because a practiced accuser learns your particular triggers and uses them precisely. The phrase that undoes you, the accusation that always lands, the topic that reliably produces the reaction, these are your strings, and the accuser knows them. Knowing them yourself, in advance and by name, is what lets you recognize a provocation as a provocation the instant it arrives, rather than being caught by it. When the familiar trigger comes, you can think, this is the parenting jab that always detonates me, and that recognition itself creates a sliver of space, because a provocation you can name is one you are no longer entirely inside.

Mapping your own strings takes some courage, because it means looking at the exact places you are most reactive, which are often the places you are most wounded. But the map is worth it, because a known trigger is a defused one, or at least a slowed one. When Alaris finally wrote down the three or four specific provocations his former partner used, he found that naming them drained some of their power, because he could see them coming and recognize them for what they were, engineered strikes at his known weak points, rather than experiencing each one as a fresh and overwhelming assault. The strings were still there, but his hand was no longer forced to the same note, because he knew which string was being plucked and why.

The relief of a slower self

Something worth promising, because it can motivate the practice through the hard early weeks: building the gap between provocation and reaction does not only protect you from the tactic, it makes your whole inner life calmer. A person who has been reacting on cue for years lives in a state of constant readiness for the next detonation, braced, watchful, exhausted by their own reactivity. Learning the pause does not only deny the accuser their evidence; it gives you back a measure of internal peace, because you are no longer at the mercy of every provocation, no longer living one message away from an explosion you will later regret.

This is why the work is worth it even beyond the strategic value. The reversal has probably left you feeling like a person who cannot control themselves, which feeds directly into the fear that you might be the abuser after all. Learning that you can receive a provocation and choose your response, that the surge does not have to become the reaction, is not only protective but restorative, because it gives you evidence, in your own experience, that you are not the out-of-control person the accusation describes. Alaris said that the quiet in his own chest, once he had built the pause, was almost more valuable than the way it defeated the provocations, because for the first time in years he did not feel like a bomb waiting to be set off. The skill defended him from the tactic and, at the same time, gave him back to himself. And there is a compounding effect over time: each provocation you let pass without reacting slightly lowers your baseline activation, so that the next provocation arrives at a body that is a little less primed to detonate. Reactivity feeds reactivity, and its opposite is also true, that steadiness builds steadiness, until the system that was trained into a hair trigger begins, slowly, to settle back toward calm as its resting state. The pause is not only a tool for the moment; practiced over months, it retrains the whole nervous system toward a steadiness that makes every future moment easier.

When the reaction still breaks through

It would be a false promise to suggest that you will never react again, and setting that expectation would only set you up for shame when you inevitably do. Sometimes, despite the pause and the practice, a provocation will get through, and you will react in a way you regret. When that happens, the task is not to spiral into proof of your own monstrousness, which is exactly what the reversal wants you to do with the slip. A single reaction, after a long stretch of steadiness, is a lapse, not a revelation, and treating it as evidence that all your progress was fake is the installed voice seizing its opening.

Handle the breakthrough reaction the way you would handle any lapse in a hard practice: notice it without drama, understand what provocation and what state produced it, and return to the practice without self-punishment. Research on self-compassion suggests that meeting your own lapses with kindness rather than harsh attack actually makes you more able to return to the practice and less likely to lapse again, because you are not caught in the shame spiral that itself drives reactivity (Neff, 2003). The goal was never a perfect record of composure, which no human being maintains. The goal is a strong overall pattern of not performing the part, within which the occasional slip is expected, forgiven, and learned from, rather than treated as the collapse of everything you have built.

Trying it on your own situation

Build the gap between provocation and reaction, starting now.

First, write down your strings: the specific provocations, phrases, and topics that reliably produce a reaction in you. Naming them in advance is what lets you recognize them in the moment as engineered strikes rather than fresh assaults.

Second, adopt one absolute rule: I will not respond to provocation while my body is activated. Decide in advance what you will do instead when you feel the surge, whether it is slow breathing with a long exhale, walking, or simply putting the device down and leaving the room.

Third, practice the settling technique when you are calm, so it is available when you are not. A few minutes of slow breathing, practiced daily, builds a tool your body will recognize under pressure. You cannot install the skill in the middle of the surge; you install it in the calm and draw on it in the storm.

Fourth, decide in advance how you will treat yourself on the day a provocation gets through and you react anyway, because that day will come. Write the response now, while you are calm: this was a lapse, not a revelation, and I will understand what produced it and return to the practice without punishing myself. Having this ready matters, because the moment after a slip is when the installed voice is loudest, insisting the reaction proves the accusation, and a decision made in advance is what keeps that voice from turning one hard moment into a collapse of all your progress.

A closing word of encouragement, because this is demanding work. Learning not to perform the part is among the hardest skills in this book, and also among the most freeing, because it reaches past the tactic into the quality of your daily life. Be patient with yourself as you build it. The nervous system that was trained into reactivity by sustained harm is not retrained in a week, and every pause you manage, every surge you let pass without acting, is a genuine victory even if some still get through. You are not trying to become a person who never feels the surge. You are becoming a person who feels it and does not have to obey it, and that person, steady in the gap between provocation and response, is both safe from the tactic and, at last, at peace in their own skin.

What to carry forward

The reversal fishes for your reaction because the reaction is its evidence, so the most protective skill is not performing the part it has written for you: receiving the provocation without producing the explosion. Willpower fails at the crucial moment because provocation works on the body faster than thought, and a nervous system kept in threat by sustained harm is primed to fire quickly and settle slowly (Porges, 2011; van der Kolk, 2014), which means your past reactions were physiology under deliberate attack, not a flaw in your character. The core tool is the strategic pause, the absolute rule never to respond while activated, using a long slow exhale and physical distance to let the wave crest and fall before you decide anything. Know your own strings, so a provocation named is a provocation slowed. Having learned not to perform the false self the accusation predicts, the book turns to the readers for whom some of the accusation was genuinely theirs, and how to own a real fault without accepting a false whole.

Chapter 11: If Some of It Was Yours

Valenor almost refused to apologize for a thing they had genuinely done, because they were terrified that owning it would prove the whole accusation true. They were thirty-nine, and in the course of a long, painful relationship they had, at one low point, read their partner's private messages without permission and lied about it afterward. It was real, and it was wrong, and Valenor knew it. But by the time the relationship ended, that genuine wrong had been folded into a sweeping accusation that Valenor was a controlling, abusive person, and so every time Valenor thought about apologizing for the messages, they froze, because to admit the one true thing felt like conceding the whole false story. So they admitted nothing, defended everything, and in defending the indefensible alongside the false, they lost their footing entirely. This chapter is about the way out of that trap, and it is one of the most important in the book.

Everything so far has helped you refuse a false accusation and recover from it. This chapter addresses the harder, more particular situation of the reader for whom some of the accusation was genuinely true, who did do real things they need to own. If that is you, this chapter is written with special care, because your situation is both more complicated and more hopeful than it feels. You can own what is genuinely yours, cleanly and fully, without accepting the false whole that has been built around it, and learning to do exactly that is what frees you from a trap that holds many people who were, in part, in the wrong.

Own the part, refuse the whole

The principle of this chapter is to own the part and refuse the whole. The trap that catches people who did some real harm is all-or-nothing thinking, the belief that admitting any fault means admitting every fault, that owning one true thing concedes the entire false story. This belief is false, and it is also paralyzing, because it forces an impossible choice between two lies: deny everything, including what is true, or accept everything, including what is false. The way out is to reject the all-or-nothing frame entirely, and to hold two things at once: yes, I did this specific thing and it was wrong, and no, that does not make me the person you have described or mean the pattern of harm was mine.

This is harder than either pure denial or pure surrender, and it is the only truthful path for a reader who genuinely did some wrong. It requires you to separate your real faults, which you will own, from the false character verdict, which you will refuse, and to hold that separation steadily even as the accuser insists the two are one. The two lists you built earlier are exactly this separation made concrete. Owning the part and refusing the whole is what lets you be both accountable and free, which is a combination the all-or-nothing frame says is impossible and which is, in fact, the truth about almost everyone.

Why owning a fault does not concede the story

It is worth seeing clearly why admitting a real fault does not, in logic or in truth, concede the false whole, because the fear that it does is what keeps people trapped. A specific wrong is a specific wrong. That you read the messages, or lied, or said something cruel, or reacted badly, is a fact about that particular act. It is not, by itself, evidence of a pattern of control, a campaign of abuse, or a monstrous character, because a single wrong or even several wrongs do not add up to a pattern of abuse, which, as the earlier chapters established, is about direction, power, and fear across time. The accuser needs you to believe that your one true fault proves their whole story, but the logic does not hold: a person can do a wrong thing, even a serious one, and not be the abuser in the relationship.

This matters because the reversal specifically exploits your conscience. A person with a conscience, confronted with a genuine fault, feels the pull to accept responsibility, and the reversal uses that pull, attaching the false whole to the true part so that your genuine accountability drags the false story in behind it. The defense is not to abandon your conscience and deny the fault, which corrupts you and confirms nothing good. The defense is to give your conscience a precise target: own exactly what is true, no more, and refuse to let the owning extend one inch into the false. Your integrity is served by owning the real fault. It is not served by accepting false guilt, which is not integrity at all but its counterfeit.

Making genuine repair

Where you did real harm, genuine repair is not only possible but healthy, and it is worth doing well, both for the person harmed and for your own recovery. Genuine repair has a shape: it names the specific thing clearly, without minimizing and without the vague non-apology that admits nothing, it takes responsibility for that specific thing without the reflexive shifting of blame, and it does not demand anything in return, not forgiveness, not a matching apology, not the dropping of the false accusation. You apologize for what is yours because it is right, fully and without conditions, and you leave the outcome open, because a repair offered in order to extract something is not a repair but a transaction.

The crucial discipline is that genuine repair for the real part is kept entirely separate from the false whole. You can say, clearly, I read your messages and lied about it, and that was wrong, and I am sorry, without in the same breath accepting that you were the controlling abuser of the relationship. Indeed, the cleanness of owning the real fault often clarifies the falseness of the rest, because a specific, sincere accountability for a specific act stands in sharp contrast to the sweeping, characterological accusation the reversal makes. Valenor eventually apologized for the messages and the lie, plainly and without defense, and in the same conversation declined the larger story, and found that the clean apology for the true thing actually strengthened their ability to refuse the false thing, because it demonstrated, to themselves most of all, that they were a person who owned their real faults and precisely for that reason did not need to accept invented ones.

Repair you owe versus confession the tactic wants

A caution is essential here, because the reversal can also weaponize the language of accountability, and you must be able to tell genuine repair from the false confession the tactic is angling for. Genuine repair is specific, proportionate, and freely chosen; it owns a real, identifiable act. The false confession the reversal seeks is different: it is a sweeping admission of a character or a pattern that was not yours, extracted under pressure, often vague, and used immediately as further proof of the reversed story. The accuser may push you toward this false confession, insisting that real accountability means admitting you were the abuser, that anything less is denial. It is not. Admitting to something you did not do is not accountability; it is capitulation to the tactic wearing accountability's clothes.

The test is whether the admission is true and specific, or false and sweeping. Owning that you read the messages is genuine repair. Admitting that you were the abusive, controlling partner of the relationship, when the pattern of harm ran the other way, is the false confession, and you should refuse it as firmly as you own the real fault. Keep the two lists in view. The first list, your genuine faults, is where repair belongs, and you should make it fully. The second list, the false whole, is where refusal belongs, no matter how strongly the accuser insists that owning the first requires accepting the second. Holding both, repairing the real and refusing the false, is the mature and truthful position, and it is available to you no matter what you actually did wrong.

How clean accountability makes you stronger

There is a counterintuitive truth at the heart of this chapter that deserves to be drawn out: owning your genuine faults cleanly does not weaken your position against the false accusation, it strengthens it. People trapped in all-or-nothing thinking assume that admitting anything hands the accuser ammunition, and so they defend everything, including the indefensible, which is precisely what makes them look evasive and embattled. The person who can say plainly, this specific thing was mine and I own it, and this sweeping thing was not, demonstrates something the accuser cannot: the capacity for real accountability, which is the very thing the reversal is designed to avoid.

This has a practical effect on how you are perceived and, more importantly, on how you perceive yourself. To any fair observer, a person who owns real faults and refuses false ones reads as truthful, while a person who denies everything reads as evasive, and the reversal actually benefits when you deny the true parts, because your obvious evasion on the real fault makes your denial of the false whole look equally unreliable. Clean accountability breaks that. And for your own recovery it is even more important, because owning what was genuinely yours is what lets you set it down. Guilt that is faced and repaired can be released; guilt that is denied festers, and guilt that is falsely inflated to include the whole accusation crushes. Valenor found that the clean apology, far from proving the accusation, was the thing that finally let them stop carrying both the real guilt and the false, because the real had been handled and the false could now be clearly seen as separate.

When you cannot make direct repair

Sometimes the person you genuinely wronged is someone you cannot or should not contact, because the relationship is over, because contact would not be safe or wise, or because an approach would be unwelcome or would reopen harm. In these cases, the impulse to make repair can leave you stuck, feeling that without the other person's participation you cannot discharge a genuine debt. It helps to know that repair is not only something enacted between two people; much of its value is in what it does in you, and that part remains available even when direct contact is not.

You can name the fault fully to yourself and to a trusted person, take genuine responsibility for it in your own reckoning, and, where the harm cannot be repaired to the person directly, commit to the change that the fault calls for, becoming, in your conduct going forward, a person who does not do that thing again. This inner repair, sometimes called making amends through changed conduct rather than through direct approach, is real accountability, and for some situations it is the only appropriate form, because forcing a direct repair on someone who does not want contact can itself be a further imposition. The point is that owning a genuine fault does not require the other person's cooperation any more than closure did. You can be fully accountable for your real faults through truthful self-reckoning and changed conduct, whatever the other person does, which means the accountability this chapter asks of you is always within your reach.

Trying it on your own situation

Practice owning the part while refusing the whole, on real material.

First, return to your two lists and look hard at the first one, the genuine faults. For each, write a clean, specific ownership: this thing, which I did, was wrong. Notice that naming it precisely does not require accepting anything on the second list.

Second, for any repair you genuinely owe, draft it in the clean form: the specific act named, responsibility taken without blame-shifting, no demand attached. Then check it against the false whole, and make sure not one inch of the repair concedes the invented story. Read it aloud and listen for the two failure modes: the vague non-apology that owns nothing, and the over-apology that spills past the specific act into accepting the false character. A clean repair sits between them, owning exactly what is true and stopping there.

Third, write the sentence that holds both at once, your version of: I did these specific things and they were wrong and I own them, and I was not the abuser you have described, and the pattern of harm was not mine. That sentence is the whole of this chapter, and it is the mature position the all-or-nothing trap says you cannot have.

Fourth, if the person you genuinely wronged is someone you cannot or should not contact, plan the inner form of repair instead: name the fault fully to yourself and a trusted person, take real responsibility for it in your own reckoning, and commit to the specific change in your conduct that the fault calls for. Write down what becoming a person who does not do that thing again actually looks like in practice. This is genuine accountability, and it is entirely within your reach, requiring nothing from anyone else.

A closing word to the reader this chapter was written for. If you came to these pages carrying real guilt alongside the false accusation, please hear this clearly: the fact that you did some genuine wrong does not make the accusation true, and it does not make you the abuser. It makes you a human being who, like nearly everyone, has done things they regret, inside a situation where those regrets were seized and inflated into a false identity. Own what is yours, fully and cleanly, because that is integrity and because it will set you free. And refuse what is not yours, firmly and without apology, because accepting false guilt is not virtue but surrender. You can be a person with real faults and not be the monster you were called. That is not a contradiction. It is the truth about you, and about most people, and holding it is the mature ground on which the rest of your recovery is built.

Where this leaves you

For the reader who genuinely did some wrong, the trap is all-or-nothing thinking, the belief that owning any fault concedes every fault, and the way out is to own the part and refuse the whole. A specific wrong, even a serious one, is not by itself a pattern of abuse, which is about direction, power, and fear over time, so admitting a real fault does not, in logic or truth, concede the false story, however hard the reversal works to attach the whole to the part by exploiting your conscience. Make genuine repair where you owe it, specific and proportionate and freely chosen, and keep it entirely separate from the false whole, distinguishing the repair you owe from the sweeping false confession the tactic wants extracted from you (Neff, 2003). Holding both, repairing the real and refusing the false, is the truthful and mature position, and it clears the way for the deepest work remaining, the rebuilding of trust in your own character, which the next chapter takes up.

Chapter 12: Rebuilding a Self You Can Trust

Noélin rebuilt herself the way you would rebuild trust with a person you had wrongly doubted: slowly, and on evidence. She was forty-one, and by the time she was free of the relationship that had rewritten her, the deepest damage was not to her circumstances but to her sense of herself. She no longer trusted her own character. When she was kind, a voice asked whether she was really being manipulative. When she was firm, the voice asked whether she was being controlling, the very word that had been used against her. She had internalized the accusation so thoroughly that she had become her own accuser, unable to do the smallest thing without interrogating her own motives for the badness she had been taught to assume was there. This chapter is about how she came back from that, and how you can, because the recovery of a self you can trust is the deepest work this book contains, and it is the point of everything that came before.

Everything so far has helped you understand the reversal, weigh the accusation, respond to it, and handle the people around it. This final chapter of the book's main work turns to the injury underneath all of it: the damage to your relationship with yourself. Being named the abuser, especially over time, can corrode your basic trust in your own character, leaving you unable to act without suspicion of your own motives. Rebuilding that trust is possible, and like all trust that has been broken, it is rebuilt not by insistence but by evidence, gathered patiently over time, until you can once again rely on your own sense of who you are.

Trust rebuilt by evidence

The principle of this chapter is that self-trust is rebuilt by evidence, not by insistence. You cannot simply decide to trust yourself again, any more than you could decide to trust a person who had hurt you; the trust has to be earned back, even from yourself, through accumulated evidence of your actual character. This is oddly hopeful, because it gives you something to do other than wait for the feeling to change. You gather evidence. You notice, and record, the moments when your conduct reflects the person you actually are, kind, fair, careful, decent, until the weight of that accumulated evidence begins to outweigh the installed accusation, and your trust in yourself is rebuilt on a foundation of observed fact rather than on either the accusation or a forced positive thinking that never quite convinces.

This approach works where insistence fails because it engages the same faculty the accusation corrupted: your capacity to judge your own character from evidence. The accusation did not just assert you were bad; it trained you to read all your own conduct as evidence of badness, so that even your kindness looked like manipulation. Rebuilding trust by evidence retrains that faculty in the other direction, teaching you to read your conduct accurately again. It is slow, because trust is always slow to rebuild, but it is reliable, because it is grounded in what you actually do rather than in what you or anyone else asserts about you.

Recovering from the installed accuser

The particular difficulty many people face is that they have internalized the accuser so completely that they now do the accusing themselves, interrogating their every motive for the badness they were taught to assume. Recovery here begins with recognizing this internalized accuser as a foreign installation, not your own judgment, the same recognition the earlier chapter on self-doubt developed, now applied to the ongoing work of living. When the voice questions your motive for a kind act, you learn to notice it, name it as the installed accuser rather than your conscience, and decline to accept its interrogation as legitimate. Recovery from trauma of this kind involves, in part, reclaiming authority over your own inner life from the voice that colonized it (Herman, 1992).

This is not a single act but a practice, repeated over months, of catching the internalized accuser and refusing its authority, until it quiets for lack of agreement. Alongside the refusal, there is a gentler move that is just as important: meeting yourself with the care you would offer a friend who had been through what you have been through. Harsh self-attack, the mode the accusation trained into you, keeps you locked in the accuser's frame; self-compassion, treating yourself with the ordinary kindness you would extend to anyone suffering, loosens that frame and creates room for a truer self-assessment (Neff, 2003). You are not indulging yourself by being kind to yourself; you are refusing the accuser's method, which was cruelty, and replacing it with the care that actually allows accurate sight.

Reclaiming your anger and grieving your losses

Two emotional currents usually need to move as part of this recovery, and both are easy to block. The first is anger, appropriate anger, at what was done to you. Many people in your position have had their anger pathologized so thoroughly, treated as proof of their dangerousness, that they have learned to suppress it entirely, which leaves them unable to feel the legitimate outrage that would help restore their sense of proportion. Reclaiming appropriate anger, the ordinary human response to being harmed and falsely accused, is part of recovering a self that knows it was wronged. This anger is not the dangerous force the accusation called it; it is the healthy signal that a boundary was violated, and letting yourself feel it, without acting on it destructively, is part of coming back.

The second current is grief, because there is a great deal to mourn: the relationship you hoped you had, the version of yourself you lost for a while, the people who fell away, the years the whole ordeal consumed. Recovery includes mourning these losses rather than rushing past them, because grief that is felt can move through and settle, while grief that is denied stays lodged and blocks the recovery behind it (Herman, 1992). Letting yourself grieve what the reversal cost you is not self-pity; it is the honoring of a real loss, and it is part of how you come out the other side. The body holds what is not felt, and releasing it, at your own pace and often with help, is part of the physical work of recovery that reconnects you to yourself (van der Kolk, 2014).

When to bring in a professional

This chapter, and this book, can orient you and give you tools, but the deep recovery of a self that has been damaged by sustained harm is often work that benefits from a skilled professional, and there is no failure in needing one. A good therapist can help you distinguish the installed accuser from your own judgment, hold the grief and anger without being overwhelmed, and rebuild self-trust in a supported way that is difficult to achieve in isolation. This is especially so if you are experiencing symptoms that interfere with daily functioning, such as persistent inability to sleep, pervasive hopelessness, or thoughts of harming yourself, any of which is a clear reason to reach for professional help without delay.

This book is a companion to that work, not a replacement for it. Reading and applying these tools may carry you a long way, and for some readers it may be enough; for many, it will be most powerful alongside the support of a qualified professional who can attend to what a book cannot. Reaching for that help is not evidence that you are as damaged as the accusation claimed. It is evidence that you are taking your own recovery seriously, which is exactly what a person worth trusting does. The goal, professional support or not, is the same: to come back to a self you can rely on, one accurate observation at a time.

The self that was there before, and the self you are becoming

Two versions of you can help anchor this rebuilding, and it is worth calling on both. The first is the self that was there before the accusation, the person you were and were known to be across a whole life before this relationship rewrote you. That self is not a fiction the installed voice can erase; it is a matter of record, held in your own memory and in the memory of people who knew you. Calling that earlier self to mind, recalling how you actually treated people across years, is a way of reminding yourself that the accusation describes a period and a distortion, not the truth of your character. You were someone before this, and that someone is evidence.

The second is the self you are becoming through the very work of recovery. Every time you own a real fault cleanly, refuse a false one, regulate a reaction, tend a loyal friend, or meet your own suffering with kindness, you are not only recovering the old self but building a new one, arguably stronger than before, because it has been tested and has learned. Noélin came to see that she was not simply trying to get back to who she had been, but becoming someone who could no longer be so easily rewritten, because she now understood the tactic, trusted her own evidence over the accusation, and knew how to hold her ground. The recovery was not only a restoration; it was a strengthening, and the person on the far side of it was harder to knock down than the person who had first been knocked down. You are not only healing back to where you were. You are becoming someone the reversal would find much more difficult to catch.

Patience with a slow return

A word about pace, because impatience with recovery is itself a way the accusation keeps its grip. Self-trust that took years to damage does not return in weeks, and the slowness can feel like failure, like proof that the damage was justified or permanent. It is neither. Rebuilding trust with yourself follows the same slow logic as rebuilding trust with anyone: it accumulates through repeated evidence over time, and it cannot be rushed by force of will any more than you could force a wronged friend to trust you again overnight. The days when the old doubt returns in full are not relapses that erase your progress; they are the ordinary texture of a long recovery, and they grow fewer and less total as the evidence accumulates.

Expecting the slowness protects you from a particular trap, in which you take the persistence of self-doubt as evidence that it was accurate all along. It is not. The doubt persists because it was deeply installed, and its fading is gradual because that is how deep installations fade. Measure your recovery not by whether the doubt has vanished, which sets you up to feel like you are failing, but by whether the evidence of your real character is accumulating and whether, over months, the doubt is a little less able to run the whole show. Noélin marked her progress not by good days, which came and went, but by the slow growth of the record she kept and by the gradual shift in which voice she believed when they disagreed. The return was slow, and it was real, and the slowness was not a verdict but simply the pace at which a self comes home.

Trying it on your own situation

Begin rebuilding self-trust on evidence, patiently.

First, start a record of your real character: small, specific moments when your conduct reflected the person you actually are, the kindness, the fairness, the restraint. Add to it regularly. You are gathering the evidence that will, over time, outweigh the installed accusation.

Second, when the internalized accuser questions your motives, practice naming it and declining its authority: that is the installed accuser, not my judgment, and I do not accept its interrogation. Pair the refusal with a kinder self-assessment, the one you would offer a friend.

Third, let one blocked emotion move this week, safely: allow yourself the appropriate anger at what was done, or the grief for what was lost, ideally with a trusted person or a professional alongside you. Feeling what was frozen is part of coming back to yourself.

Fourth, measure your recovery by the right yardstick. Rather than asking whether the self-doubt is gone, which sets you up to feel like you are failing, track two things over time: whether the record of your real character is growing, and whether, when the old doubt and your own judgment disagree, you are a little more often able to believe your judgment. Note these monthly, not daily, because the change is slow and only visible across weeks. Measuring the right things keeps the ordinary slowness of recovery from being read as failure, and lets you see the real progress that a day-to-day view would miss.

A closing word, and it is the one this whole book has been moving toward. You were named the abuser, and for a while, perhaps a long while, you may have half-believed it, and it damaged the most important relationship you have, the one with yourself. The work of coming back from that is slow and it is real and it is yours to do, one accurate observation at a time, with help where you need it and patience always. The accusation was loud, and it got inside, and it tried to convince you that you could not trust your own heart. It was wrong. You can rebuild a self you rely on, grounded in the evidence of who you actually are, and when you have, the accusation will have lost the only power it ever truly had over you, which was your agreement. That self, rebuilt on evidence and held with care, is the ground you will stand on for the rest of your life, and no reversal can take it once you have earned it back.

What to carry forward

Self-trust is rebuilt not by insistence but by evidence, gathered patiently until the weight of your actual conduct outweighs the installed accusation and you can rely on your own sense of who you are again. Recover authority over your inner life from the internalized accuser by naming it as a foreign installation rather than your conscience, and pair that refusal with self-compassion, since cruelty keeps you in the accuser's frame while kindness allows accurate sight (Herman, 1992; Neff, 2003). Let your appropriate anger and your genuine grief move rather than blocking them, because felt emotion settles while denied emotion stays lodged and blocks recovery (van der Kolk, 2014), and bring in a skilled professional for the deep work, without shame, especially if daily functioning is affected. Coming back to a self you can trust, one accurate observation at a time, is the point of everything this book has done, and the final chapter gathers it all into a way of carrying the accusation lightly, for good.

Chapter 13: Living Named and Free

Sevrin keeps a folded page in his wallet, and he has read it in more parking lots than he can count. He was forty-five, and by the time he reached the far side of the ordeal, he understood that being named the abuser was not something he would ever fully undo. Some people would always believe the story. The accusation would surface again, at a school event, in a mutual friend's careless remark, in his own mind on a bad night. What changed was not that the accusation disappeared, but that he had built a way of carrying it that did not cost him himself. The folded page was part of that: his own conclusions, in his own hand, ready for the moments the old weight returned. He had stopped waiting to be cleared. He had learned, instead, to live named and free.

This final chapter gathers everything the book has built into something portable, a way of carrying the accusation without being ruled by it, for the long term. You may never receive the vindication you deserve. The accusation may never be formally withdrawn, the turned people may never fully return, the accuser may never admit the truth. This chapter is about living well anyway, not in denial of the accusation, but in a settled relationship to it, where it is something that was said about you rather than the truth of you, something you carry lightly rather than something that carries you. That is the freedom that was available all along, and this chapter is how you keep it.

Carry it lightly

The principle of this chapter is to carry it lightly, which does not mean pretending it did not happen or does not hurt, but holding it in its proper place, as a claim that was made about you and not as the fact of who you are. A weight carried close to the body, gripped tight, exhausts you; the same weight, set in its proper place and carried with the right posture, can be borne for a long way. The accusation is a weight you may carry for years, and how you hold it determines whether it breaks you or simply accompanies you. Carrying it lightly is the posture that lets you walk a long way without being crushed, and it is built from everything the book has given you: the name for the tactic, the fair conclusion about your conduct, the response skills, the recovered self.

This posture is a choice you make repeatedly, not a state you arrive at once. There will be days the weight drags, when the accusation surfaces and pulls you back toward the old collapse, and on those days you return, deliberately, to the practices and conclusions you have built, and you re-establish the lighter hold. Living named and free is not the absence of the accusation from your life; it is a practiced, repeatable way of carrying it that keeps it from governing you. You will get better at it with time, until the reach for the lighter hold becomes nearly automatic, and the accusation, though still present, becomes something in the background of your life rather than its center.

Your portable plan

Everything in this book can be gathered into a short personal plan you carry, literally or in memory, and return to whenever the accusation resurfaces. Your plan has a few elements, each drawn from a chapter you have worked through. It has your grounded conclusion from the self-check, the sentence that owns what was real and refuses what was false, ready to outrank the doubt when it surges. It has your response rules, the narrow calm answer and the absolute pause, ready for the next provocation or accusation. It has your few anchors, the people who see you, and your reminder to reach for them rather than withdraw. It has your line between genuine repair and false confession, so you never again confuse owning a fault with accepting the false whole. And it has your reality reminder, the record of your real character, ready to set against the installed voice.

The value of gathering these into one place is that the moments you most need them are the moments you are least able to reconstruct them, when the accusation has surfaced and the old collapse is pulling at you and your clear thinking is the first thing to go. A plan prepared in a settled hour and kept ready, folded in a wallet or fixed in memory, is what carries you through the unsettled ones. Sevrin's folded page was exactly this, a few lines that took him minutes to write and years to fully trust, that he could pull out in a parking lot before walking into a room where the accusation might be waiting, and that returned him, each time, to the ground he had built. You do not have to win the moment. You have to return to your plan, and let it hold you until the moment passes. This is a gentler standard than the one you have probably been holding yourself to, and it is worth taking in. You do not have to be strong in the moment the accusation lands. You do not have to have the perfect response, or feel calm, or win anything. You have to do one small, achievable thing: reach for the plan you prepared when you were steady, and let it carry you the short distance to the other side of the moment. Strength, here, is not a feeling you summon; it is a structure you built in advance and now simply lean on, and leaning on it is not weakness but exactly the use it was made for.

When the accusation resurfaces

It helps to expect the resurfacing, so that it does not undo you each time. The accusation will return, in a stray comment, an official form that asks an old question, a memory that ambushes you, a bad night when the installed voice finds new fuel. Expecting these returns strips them of some of their power, because a resurfacing you anticipated is one you can meet with your plan rather than one that catches you defenseless. When it comes, you do not have to relitigate the whole thing or prove yourself again. You reach for your conclusion, your practices, your anchors, and you carry the weight through the moment with the posture you have built.

Over time, the resurfacing tends to lose its intensity, not because the accusation changes, but because your relationship to it does. What once produced days of collapse comes to produce an hour of discomfort, then a passing pang, as the practices become more automatic and the recovered self more solid. This is what healing actually looks like in a situation that does not offer clean vindication: not the disappearance of the accusation, but the steady shrinking of its power to move you, until it becomes a fact about your past that you carry without strain, one chapter of a life that has many others. Sevrin found that the parking-lot moments grew shorter and rarer over the years, and that the folded page, though he still carried it, was one he needed to read less and less, because its conclusions had finally become his own settled sense of himself. That is the destination this whole book has been walking toward: not a day when the accusation is formally undone, which may never come, but a day when its conclusions no longer live outside you on a folded page, because they have become simply how you know yourself. The plan is scaffolding. You build it because you need it, and you lean on it for as long as you need it, and one distant day you may find you have quietly become the thing the scaffolding was holding up, a person whose settled knowledge of their own character no longer needs to be reached for because it is simply, steadily there.

Freedom without vindication

The hardest and most liberating idea in this chapter deserves to be stated plainly, because so much of your suffering has been tied to waiting for the thing that would make it right. You have probably been waiting, on some level, to be vindicated: for the accuser to admit the truth, for the turned people to see clearly, for the record to be corrected, for the world to finally acknowledge what really happened. That vindication may never come, and if your freedom depends on it, your freedom is hostage to people and events you do not control. The move this whole book has been building toward is to stop making your peace conditional on a vindication that may never arrive, and to build a freedom that does not require it.

This is not resignation, and it is not giving up on the truth. It is refusing to let the absence of external vindication keep you imprisoned in the accusation. You know what happened. You have done the fair examination and reached your grounded conclusion. You have rebuilt a self you can trust on the evidence of your actual character. None of that required the accuser's admission or the world's acknowledgment, and none of your ongoing freedom does either. Sevrin never got his vindication; the story about him persists in certain rooms to this day. What he got instead was the discovery that he could be free without it, that his settled knowledge of himself did not need ratification from the people who had believed the reversal. The freedom that needs no vindication is the only kind that cannot be withheld from you, and it is the kind this book has been placing, piece by piece, within your reach.

A self the reversal cannot reach

There is a particular strength that comes out the far side of this experience, and it is worth naming as encouragement for the long walk. A person who has been named the abuser, has faced the terrifying question of whether it was true, has examined themselves with courage, and has come back to a grounded self, is far harder to knock down than they were before. You now know the tactic by name. You know your own conduct, fairly assessed. You know how to respond, how to regulate, how to tell real repair from false confession, how to rebuild trust in yourself on evidence. These are not only tools for surviving what happened; they are a kind of armor against its ever having the same power over you again.

This is the strange gift buried in a terrible experience, and it does not excuse or justify what was done to you, but it is real nonetheless. The reversal tried to make you doubt your own character, and in fighting your way back to a grounded sense of yourself, you built something sturdier than what you had before it started, a self held together not by others' opinions but by your own fair knowledge of who you are. That self is the one thing the reversal set out to destroy and, in the end, could not, because you rebuilt it on ground the tactic cannot reach: the evidence of your actual conduct, weighed by your own recovered judgment, and held with care. Carry that lightly, and walk on. The accusation is behind you now, or beside you at most, and the road ahead is yours. You spent long enough walking backward, watching the accusation, trying to answer it, waiting to be cleared of it. You are allowed to turn around now and walk forward, toward the ordinary, unremarkable, precious business of a life, and to let the accusation recede behind you at the pace it will, without giving it one more backward glance than you must.

Trying it on your own situation

Assemble your portable plan and prepare to carry it.

First, write your one-page plan, gathering the elements from across the book: your grounded conclusion, your response rules, your few anchors, your line between repair and false confession, and your reality reminder. Keep it somewhere you can reach it.

Second, decide in advance how you will use the plan when the accusation resurfaces: where you keep it, when you will read it, and what you will do instead of collapsing into the old response. A plan you have decided how to use is one that will actually hold you.

Third, name the life you are carrying the plan toward. The plan is not the point; it is what frees you to live. Write down one part of your life, beyond the accusation, that you are reclaiming, and let that be the direction you walk while carrying the weight lightly.

Fourth, write one sentence that releases you from waiting for vindication, your version of: I know what happened, I have done the fair examination, and my freedom does not depend on anyone else admitting the truth. Keep it with your plan. On the days you catch yourself waiting again for the accuser to confess or the world to see clearly, read it, and return your attention to the life in front of you, which is the one thing that was always yours to build regardless of what anyone else ever acknowledges.

A closing word for the road. This has been a hard book about a hard thing, and if you have worked through it, you have done something courageous: you have faced the possibility that you were the villain, examined it fairly, and come out holding a truer and steadier sense of yourself than the accusation allowed. Carry your plan, tend your few, keep your practices, and walk on into the life that is waiting past this. The weight may travel with you for a while yet, but you know now how to hold it lightly, and lightly held, it will not keep you from the road. You were named. You are not what you were named. And you are free to go and live as the person you actually are, which is, and always was, the truth the reversal could not touch.

What to carry forward

Living named and free means carrying the accusation lightly, holding it in its proper place as a claim that was made about you rather than the fact of who you are, a posture chosen repeatedly rather than a state arrived at once. Gather everything the book has built into a short portable plan, your grounded conclusion, your response rules, your few anchors, your line between genuine repair and false confession, and your reality reminder, prepared in a settled hour and kept ready for the unsettled ones. Expect the accusation to resurface, and meet each return with your plan rather than a fresh collapse, watching its power to move you shrink over the years as the practices become automatic and the recovered self becomes solid. You may never be formally cleared, and you can be free anyway, which was the point all along. The conclusion that follows speaks to that freedom directly, and to the truth the whole book has been for: you are not the reversal.

Conclusion: You Are Not the Reversal

At the start of this book, you wrote down a sentence: the accusation as it was put to you, in the words that were used. I want you to find that sentence now, at the end, and read it again, because you are a different reader than the one who wrote it. When you wrote it, the accusation may have felt like a verdict, something true and terrible about who you are. I hope that by now it reads differently, as what it actually is: a claim, made by someone with a reason to make it, using a recognizable tactic, that you have examined fairly and found does not fit. The words on the page have not changed. You have.

That is the whole movement of this book, from a person shattered and defined by the accusation to a person who understands the reversal, knows their own character, and is no longer ruled by what they were called. We began by naming the tactic and seeing that being cast as the abuser is its sharpest move, not a fair account of your conduct. We faced the question underneath everything, whether the accusation might be true, and answered it not with reassurance but with a rigorous self-check that owns what is real and refuses what is false. We saw why the doubt felt so overwhelmingly true, how it was installed through betrayal and repetition, and we learned to read the pattern of a relationship through direction, power, and fear rather than through the isolated incidents the reversal weaponizes.

From there the work turned outward and then back in. We faced the painful reality that others often believe the reversed story, and learned to stay steady when disbelieved rather than confirming the picture through frantic defense. We learned to answer the charge and not the shame, to face the accuser while releasing the impossible hope of being understood, and to keep and tend the few who still see us. We learned not to perform the part the accusation predicts, regulating the body so the provocation does not become the reaction.

We faced, with particular care, the situation of the reader who did some genuine wrong, and learned to own the part while refusing the whole. And we turned to the deepest work, rebuilding a self we can trust on the evidence of our actual character, and gathering everything into a portable way of living named and free.

Underneath all of it has been a single truth, the one this conclusion is here to state plainly: you are not the reversal. The reversal is something that was done to you, a tactic aimed at your identity, and it depends for its power on two things, your self-doubt and the absence of any clear account of what really happened. You have taken both away from it. You have replaced the self-doubt with a grounded conclusion reached by fair examination, and you have replaced the absence of an account with a clear reading of the pattern and a record of your real character. Stripped of those two supports, the reversal loses its hold, not because the accuser stops making it, but because you have stopped supplying the agreement it needed.

There is a freedom in this that does not depend on anything you cannot control. You may never be vindicated. The accuser may never admit the truth, the people who turned may never fully return, the story may persist in certain rooms for the rest of your life. And you can be free anyway, because the freedom this book has been building was never the freedom of being cleared by others. It was the freedom of knowing, on the evidence, who you actually are, and no longer needing the accuser's admission or the world's acknowledgment to hold that knowledge steady. That freedom cannot be withheld from you by anyone, because you build it and you keep it, out of courage and a fair method and the patient accumulation of evidence.

So carry your conclusion, tend your few, keep your practices, and walk on. Read your plan when the accusation resurfaces, and let it hold you until the moment passes, which it will, more quickly each time. Be patient with the slow return of trust in yourself, and reach for help when you need it, without shame. And when the old voice comes at night to tell you that you are the monster you were called, meet it with the truth you have earned: that you asked the hard question, looked without flinching, owned what was yours, refused what was not, and came back to a self you can trust. You were named the abuser. You are not the abuser. You are not the reversal. You are the person who saw the tactic clearly, reclaimed your story, and walked free of a name that was never the truth of you. Name the tactic. Reclaim your story. The rest of your life is waiting, and it is yours.

Appendix A: The Am I the Abuser Self-Check

This self-check gathers the questions from Chapter 3 into one place, so you can return to it whenever the doubt resurfaces. It is not a diagnostic instrument and it cannot determine the facts of your situation. It is a structured way to examine your own conduct with care, and its value depends entirely on your willingness to answer truthfully rather than to reach a predetermined verdict in either direction. Work through it slowly, in writing, ideally more than once and ideally with a trusted person or a professional alongside you.

First, the willingness question. Are you willing to consider that some of the accusation might be true. A person running the reversal is characteristically unwilling to examine themselves at all; the very fact that you are asking the question in good faith already distinguishes you from the tactic you fear you might be running. Notice your willingness, and notice too any impulse to use this check to convict yourself of everything, which is its own kind of avoidance.

Second, the specific-behavior question. Setting aside character verdicts and labels entirely, what specific things did you actually do. Write them as concrete acts, not as summaries or judgments. The reversal traffics in sweeping character claims; accurate self-examination traffics in specific behaviors. This question moves you from the fog of you are abusive to the firmer ground of here is what I actually did, which is the only ground on which a fair judgment can be made.

Third, the origin question. For each specific act, what came before it. Was it a first move or a response, part of a pattern you initiated or a reaction to something being done to you. This question does not excuse genuine wrongs, but it does distinguish an act that originates harm from an act that responds to it, which is central to telling reactive defense from a pattern of abuse.

Fourth, the pattern question. Looking across time rather than at single incidents, what is the direction of the overall pattern. Who, across the relationship, held and used power over the other; who was afraid of whom; whose behavior was controlling the other's. A pattern of abuse is about direction, power, and fear over time, not about isolated incidents, and this question asks you to assess the whole rather than the moments the accusation isolates.

Fifth, the fear question. In the relationship, were you afraid, and of what. Did you change your behavior to avoid the other person's reactions, monitor your words to keep the peace, feel controlled or diminished over time. Fear is one of the clearest signals of the actual direction of harm, and it frequently points the opposite way from the accusation.

Having worked through these, write two lists. The first is the genuine faults, the specific things you did that were wrong, which you will own and, where appropriate, repair. The second is the false whole, the sweeping character verdict and the reversed pattern, which you will refuse. Almost no one who works through this check in good faith finds the two lists to be the same, and the discipline of keeping them separate is the practical heart of this book.

Appendix B: Reactive Defense or a Pattern of Harm

This guide gathers the discernment tools from Chapters 2 and 5 for telling reactive defense from a genuine pattern of harm. It is meant to help a genuine target see their situation clearly. It is not a way to excuse a real pattern of harm, and if the truthful application of these tests points toward your own conduct, the right response is accountability, not evasion.

Consider direction. Across the whole relationship, not in single moments, in which direction did control run. Who set the terms the other adapted to, whose moods the household organized itself around, whose displeasure the other worked to avoid. Reactive defense is the response of the controlled; a pattern of harm is the conduct of the one controlling.

Consider power. Who held and used power over the other, in decisions, money, freedom, and the ability to define what was real. A single angry outburst from a person who otherwise held little power in the relationship is a different thing from the same outburst by the person who held most of it, even though they may look identical in isolation, which is exactly why the reversal isolates them.

Consider fear. Who was afraid of whom. Fear is difficult to fake across time and hard to hide from yourself once you look. If you were the one afraid, monitoring, walking on eggshells, that points strongly to your having been the target rather than the source, whatever the accusation says.

Consider origin. Did your worst behavior tend to originate harm or respond to it. A reaction, even an ugly one, that arose in response to being harmed is reactive defense, poorly executed perhaps, but not the same as a pattern that initiates. This distinction does not make every reaction acceptable, but it does locate it accurately.

A caution, kept deliberately in view: relationships can be genuinely mutual, with both people contributing harm, and in a real mutual situation the truthful work is to own your real part without either accepting a false whole or using mutuality to dodge accountability. And in the rare case where these tests point toward your own conduct as the pattern, the right response is the accountability Chapter 11 describes, not a search for a more comfortable answer.

Appendix C: The Calm Response Template

This template gathers the response discipline from Chapters 6 and 7 into a form you can use when an accusation must be answered. Its logic is simple: answer the charge, not the shame; keep the response narrow, factual, and unemotional; take the emotional pressure elsewhere.

Before responding at all, wait. Do not answer while activated. Let the surge pass, which it will, and decide whether a response is even needed, since many accusations, especially pure character attacks, are best met with no response at all.

If a response is needed, include only these elements. A brief, factual correction of any specific, answerable claim: this specific thing did not happen; here, in a sentence, is what did. A calm decline of anything that is not a specific answerable claim: I am not going to argue my character. Nothing else. No defense of who you are, no counter-attack, no plea to be understood, no emotional escalation.

Before sending, check the response against three questions. Does it answer only specific claims, or has it drifted into defending your character. Is it free of heat, counter-attack, and pleading. Have you put the emotional pressure somewhere else first, into a notebook, a friend, or a professional, rather than into this reply. If the response fails any of these, revise it or do not send it.

Remember that the smallest adequate response is almost always the best one, and that no response at all is frequently best of all. The goal is not to win the exchange but to decline to perform the role the accusation assigns you.

Appendix D: Genuine Repair or False Confession

This guide gathers the distinction from Chapter 11, for readers who did some genuine wrong and need to own it without accepting a false whole. Use it to tell a repair you should make from a confession the tactic wants to extract.

Genuine repair is specific: it names a real, identifiable act. False confession is sweeping: it admits a character or a pattern rather than an act.

Genuine repair is proportionate: it owns the actual wrong at its actual size. False confession is inflated: it accepts responsibility for far more than you did, up to the whole reversed story.

Genuine repair is freely chosen: it comes from your own conscience. False confession is extracted: it is produced under pressure, to end an interrogation or appease an accuser.

Genuine repair is true: you did the thing you are owning. False confession is false: you are admitting to something that was not yours, or accepting a pattern that ran the other way.

The practical rule is to keep your two lists in view and let each guide the right response. The first list, your genuine faults, is where repair belongs; make it fully, specifically, and without conditions. The second list, the false whole, is where refusal belongs; decline it as firmly as you own the first, no matter how strongly you are told that real accountability requires accepting it. Owning a real fault does not require confessing to a false identity, and the difference between the two is the difference between integrity and surrender.

Appendix E: A Record of Your Real Character

This appendix supports the practice from Chapter 12, of rebuilding self-trust on evidence. Its premise is that self-trust returns not through insistence but through the patient accumulation of accurate observations of your actual conduct, gathered until their weight outbalances the installed accusation.

Keep an ongoing record. It can be a notebook, a note on your phone, a document, anything you will actually use. Into it, regularly, put small, specific, true observations of your own conduct that reflect the person you actually are: a moment you were kind when you did not have to be, a time you were fair to someone who was not fair to you, an instance of restraint, patience, generosity, or care. Specific and true is the whole point; this is not positive thinking or affirmation, which the installed voice easily dismisses, but a record of real evidence it cannot fairly wave away.

When the internalized accuser questions your motives, turning your kindness into manipulation and your firmness into control, bring it to the record. Set its sweeping claim against the specific accumulated evidence of how you actually behave. Over months, the weight of accurate observation begins to shift which voice you believe, not by argument but by evidence, until you can once again rely on your own sense of who you are.

Add to the record on good days and bad. On the bad days, when the accusation feels true, the record is there precisely to be read, a store of evidence gathered in clearer moments and kept ready for the moments you cannot see yourself accurately. This is how a self is rebuilt after it has been damaged: one true observation at a time, patiently, until the person on the page and the person you feel yourself to be become, at last, the same.

Appendix F: The DARVO Survival Guides

This book is part of a series that examines DARVO, the reversal tactic in which a person confronted with their own conduct responds by denying it, attacking the one who named it, and reversing the roles of victim and offender so that the person who caused harm claims to be the wronged party. Each book in the series applies this lens to a different situation, and each can be read on its own or alongside the others.

The companion volumes develop, in their own contexts, several tools this book draws on: the practice of writing for a third reader, the structured low-contact approach to an ongoing relationship, and the discipline of documentation. Readers facing the reversal inside a divorce, a custody dispute, or co-parenting with a manipulative former partner will find those situations addressed directly in the companion volumes.

If this book served you, the most useful thing you can do, beyond applying it, is to leave a truthful review where you bought it, so that others in the same painful situation can find it. Being named the abuser is an isolating experience, and many who go through it do not know there is a name for what is happening to them or a way through it. A review is how the next person finds the door.

Name the tactic. Reclaim your story.

References

Baumeister, R. F., Bratslavsky, E., Finkenauer, C., & Vohs, K. D. (2001). Bad is stronger than good. *Review of General Psychology, 5*(4), 323-370. https://doi.org/10.1037/1089-2680.5.4.323

Freyd, J. J. (1996). *Betrayal trauma: The logic of forgetting childhood abuse.* Harvard University Press.

Freyd, J. J. (1997). Violations of power, adaptive blindness, and betrayal trauma theory. *Feminism & Psychology, 7*(1), 22-32. https://doi.org/10.1177/0959353597071004

Harsey, S. J., & Freyd, J. J. (2020). Deny, attack, and reverse victim and offender (DARVO): What is the influence on perceived perpetrator and victim credibility? *Journal of Aggression, Maltreatment & Trauma, 29*(8), 897-916. https://doi.org/10.1080/10926771.2020.1774695

Harsey, S. J., Zurbriggen, E. L., & Freyd, J. J. (2017). Perpetrator responses to victim confrontation: DARVO and victim self-blame. *Journal of Aggression, Maltreatment & Trauma, 26*(6), 644-663. https://doi.org/10.1080/10926771.2017.1320777

Herman, J. L. (1992). *Trauma and recovery.* Basic Books.

Neff, K. D. (2003). Self-compassion: An alternative conceptualization of a healthy attitude toward oneself. *Self and Identity, 2*(2), 85-101. https://doi.org/10.1080/15298860309032

Porges, S. W. (2011). *The polyvagal theory: Neurophysiological foundations of emotions, attachment, communication, and self-regulation.* W. W. Norton.

Smith, C. P., & Freyd, J. J. (2014). Institutional betrayal. *American Psychologist, 69*(6), 575-587. https://doi.org/10.1037/a0037564

Stark, E. (2007). *Coercive control: How men entrap women in personal life.* Oxford University Press.

Sweet, P. L. (2019). The sociology of gaslighting. *American Sociological Review, 84*(5), 851-875. https://doi.org/10.1177/0003122419874843

van der Kolk, B. A. (2014). *The body keeps the score: Brain, mind, and body in the healing of trauma.* Viking.

About the Author

Arnold Wellington McLean is a mental health professional and researcher with an interest in trauma. His work focuses on how manipulation and betrayal affect the people subjected to them, and on turning that understanding into plain, practical guidance. He is the author of The DARVO Survival Guides, a series that helps readers name the deny, attack, reverse tactic and respond to it with clarity and self-respect.

www.ingramcontent.com/pod-product-compliance
Lightning Source LLC
LaVergne TN
LVHW050824061126
851857LV00012B/968
9798906782212